A Jewish Mother in Shangri-la

A JEWISH MOTHER IN SHANGRI-LA

———

Rosie Rosenzweig

FOREWORD BY
Sylvia Boorstein

SHAMBHALA
Boulder
2019

Shambhala Publications, Inc.
4720 Walnut Street
Boulder, Colorado 80301
www.shambhala.com

First Paperback Edition
Printed in the United States of America

♾ This edition is printed on acid-free paper that meets the
American National Standards Institute z39.48 Standard.
♻ Shambhala Publications makes every effort to print on recycled paper.
For more information please visit www.shambhala.com.

The Library of Congress catalogues the hardcover edition of this book as follows:
Rosenzweig, Rosie.
A Jewish mother in Shangri-La/Rosie Rosenzweig;
foreword by Sylvia Boorstein
p. cm.
ISBN 978-1-57062-353-0 (hardcover)
ISBN 978-1-57062-459-9 (paperback)
1. Rosenzweig, Rosie. 2. Rosenzweig, Ben, 1961– .
3. Jews—Massachusetts—Maynard—Biography. 4. Buddhist
converts from Judaism. 5. Spiritual life—Judaism.
6. Spiritual Life—Buddhism. I. Title.
F74.M46R67 1998 97-42455
296.3'9—dc21 CIP
[B]

For my husband, Sandy,
whose Hebrew name, Sholem,
describes him fully.

Contents

Foreword

BY SYLVIA BOORSTEIN

In my first telephone conversation with Rosie Rosenzweig, in which she told me about herself and her son, Ben, and her book—long before I ever saw the manuscript—I volunteered to write this foreword. I thought, "Finally! Once and for all we will be finished with the dreadful, disparaging 'Sheldon and His Mother' story, which made its rounds of American Buddhist communities for decades." I didn't know then that Sheldon would show up on the first page of Rosie's book—and it's appropriate that he does. Rosie rewrites the end to the Sheldon story with the story of her own life, and of Ben's. She offers us a new model of mother (Jewish or otherwise) with wider-than-parochial vision, as well as a model of a sincere, open-minded, dedicated spiritual life firmly rooted in ordinary family life and traditional religious community.

The Sheldon story was meant to be a joke, and lots of people laughed when they heard it, but I never found it funny. I think people laughed because it made them uneasy. I thought it trivialized: it trivialized the enormous pain so many people have felt when someone they loved seemed outside the safety of their own religious community. When I was a child, I heard hushed stories, or oblique references, to "So-and-So who married out-of-the-faith" and of their families who sat *shiva* (performed the rites of mourning for them). The joke trivializes Jewish mothers, stereotyping them as dumpily "shlepping" food and doggedly, determinedly unable to recognize their sons as mature people capable of independent choice. And the joke trivializes the many, many other Westerners—some celebrated, like Thomas Merton, but mostly just regular people looking for a serious spiritual practice—who aren't Jews, who also are eagerly studying what the Buddha taught.

Rosie liberates us from the joke forever—not in spite of telling it, but because of telling it. Because after she tells it, she tells us about herself. She tells us about her pain. "Have I failed as a mother?" "What about my ancestors?" "Will Ben be happy?" "How can I participate with my son in this Buddhist ceremony and show him and his teacher the love and respect I feel, and still not bow?" "What would happen if I bowed?" And Rosie tells us about her trip to Plum Village, Thich Nhat Hanh's community in France, and to the Himalayas—not to plead with her son to come home, but to learn from his teachers. She shares with us her running inner translation: "Okay, this means Ein Sof," "This is the blessing over food," "This is *mitzvot* [service] practice," letting us know that it is not easy for her to do this trip, that she takes comfort from her personal anchor in Judaism to assure herself that she is okay and that Ben is okay.

And as Rosie learns from Ben's teachers, she teaches them, sharing with them, kindly and respectfully, very good Jewish wisdom. We get the sense that she presents her understanding of Judaism in the genuine delight of discovering shared universal knowledge. Rosie listens to what the Buddha taught. The Buddhist teachers hear about Judaism. The reader learns from both. And the reader shares Rosie's growing awareness of what we are beginning to name as "post-parochial" or "trans-parochial" understanding: an understanding that kindness and compassion are universal and that different particular expressions of the fundamental wisdom that supports them can all be respected as valuable.

Rosie isn't the only Jewish mother to break the stereotype mold. Lots of my friends' mothers did it, too. Sarah Harding, an American teacher of Tibetan Buddhism, a Jew by birth, told me about her eighty-six-year-old grandmother who went with her by subway from South Brooklyn to Manhattan to visit her teacher, Kalu Rinpoche, when he was teaching in New York. The grandmother was very hard of hearing. Kalu Rinpoche didn't speak English. Sarah's grandmother brought cookies, Sarah translated, and they all had tea. Rosie Rosenzweig had tea with Thich Nhat Hanh and an interview with Tulku Urgyen Rinpoche in Kathmandu—and a wisdom transmission as well, which she shares with all of us. Rosie's spiritual journey, motivated by her love for her son and sustained, but not constrained, by her fidelity to her own religious tradition, inspires faith that sincere, illuminating interreligious dialogue, on behalf of all participants—on behalf of all beings—is a possibility. May it be so.

Acknowledgments

Many teachers and helpers have helped me bring this project to fruition. My husband reminds me that the opinions in this book are ones that he has heard repeatedly through our years together. So I want to thank my teachers for their teachings and the pleasure that I had hearing them. They may not remember me, but their presence influenced me greatly. If there is any merit in my conclusions in this book, may my teachers have the merit for their inspiration.

The Rebonim include: The Lubavitcher Rebbe, Rabbi Menachem Mendel Schneerson of blessed memory, whose presence stimulated awe in me, Rabbi Adin Steinsaltz, Rabbi Zalman Schachter-Shalomi, Rabbi Shlomo Carlebach, Rabbi Gedalia Fleer, Rabbi Lawrence Kushner, Rabbi Nehemia Polen, Rabbi Joseph Polak, Rabbi Eliyahu Alfasi, Rabbi Yaakov Lazaros, Rabbi Levi Fogelman, Rabbi Manis Friedman, Rabbi Laibl Wolfe, Rabbi Yitchok Aharon Korff, Rabbi Harold Kushner, Rabbi Meier Sendor, Rabbi David Zeller, Rabbi Art Green, Rabbi Cherie Kohler-Fox, and the countless teachers (including Everett Fox) at the CAJE conferences.

The Buddhist meditation and philosophy teachers include

Tulku Urgyen Rinpoche, whose memory brings me peace, Thich Nhat Hanh, whose words still teach me, Chökyi Nyima Rinpoche, Tsok Nyi Rinpoche, Alan Watts, Sylvia Boorstein, Joseph Goldstein, Larry Rosenberg, and Andrew Oldendzki.

At my age, this list should have been even longer. This also means my memory needs constant reminding about wisdom—which I get from my son, who is one of my best teachers. He has been my Buddhist guide and encyclopedia throughout this project. My fond gratitude extends to him, whose patient explanations, sometimes covering the same ground repeatedly, enrich this book beyond measure as well as my life. His devoted siblings, Rebecca and Elizabeth, as well as his brother-in-law, Joel, were good readers and their feedback was very valuable. An apology to my three grandsons, Max, Levi, and Daniel, for not having a grandmother available as often as she would have liked.

My editor, at Shambhala Publications, Kendra Crossen Burroughs, has been a wellspring of information, wisdom, and creative solutions; she saw my vision and made me make it better. In fact, everyone at Shambhala has been a pleasure to work with.

Thanks go to the publishers of *The Forward, Neshama, Lichora, Vetaher Libaynu, Genesis 2,* and *Horizons,* in which versions of some of the chapters in this book first appeared.

Without the initial encouragement from Rabbi Cherie Kohler-Fox, this book would have never been written. She saw my vision before I did.

Thank you to the many readers who supplied insight, information, and suggestions. They include Barbara Holender, Arnie Kotler, Ed Vesnesky, Judy Amtzis, Binah Schor, Ed Hoffman, Rodger Kamenetz, Joel Ziff, and of course, most of all, my husband, Sandy Rosenzweig. Without him and his wisdom, humor, availability, and affection, I could not have mustered the courage to begin the journey of this book. *Ad me-ah v'esrim.*

Finally, blessed be the Holy One, who helped me with life, sustained me, and brought me to this moment in time and space.

A Jewish Mother in Shangri-la

1

My Son the Buddhist

THE STORY OF THE JEWISH MOTHER AND THE GURU IS famous in Jewish and Buddhist circles. Shlepping her shopping bags full of chicken soup, challah, kugel, rugelach, and banana bread, this mother has traveled over land and over water, by plane, train, and bus all the way from America to Nepal. She knocks at the monastery door, desperate to see the guru. Finally a monk answers, and she asks to see the guru. The monk sends her away to complete the necessary training and pass many rigorous tests. Eventually she comes back, still shlepping her shopping bags.

Now that she has fulfilled the requirements for entry, the monk allows her in, accompanies her through the monastery, and opens the shrine-room door to reveal a forty-foot Buddha with the guru seated on a golden platform beside it. He will allow her to utter only five words to the guru. Parking her shoes, she ascends the long staircase to the golden throne, puts down her shopping bags, looks the guru in the eye, and says: "Nu, Sheldon, come home already."

In November 1984, when I used this joke as a lead in an article on Jewish meditation for a Boston newspaper called *Genesis 2*, I never dreamed that this caricature would even remotely apply to me—and that one day I would be writing a book about my travels to meet my son's Buddhist teachers and how I struggled to reconcile myself to his spiritual path.

Being a private person well suited to the meditative path, my son, Ben, would have preferred that I not write about these travels. However, as a child of immigrant parents who were illiterate in the skills of self-expression, I have worked hard to use writing as a way of realizing how I feel, what I've learned, and how to deal with life-changing events beyond my control. I hope that this process of understanding may lead me to know who I am and how to live my life. More important, writing has become a search for wisdom that may enable me to bear the vicissitudes of life. My travel journal was often blotched with tears, but I kept remembering the biblical prophecy of Malachai (3:24) that someday a spiritual force will turn the heart of the parents to the children, and the heart of the children to the parents. I struggled to hope that maybe, just maybe, such a heart-turn would occur between my son and me.

Ben is not the Sheldon in the story; he is his own person who will be what he wants to be regardless of any mold or image that I may have of him. When he was born in 1961, his bright-red hair made him seem like an exotic flashback to the Old World. We gave him the Jewish name Ya'akov, after my mother's grandfather, Ya'akov Bar Kobrin, a redhead with a red beard. Years later, the sight of Ben made my mother's aunt Zelda, exclaim: "My father lives!" I knew little about this grandfather, but I did learn that he had arranged a marriage for Aunt Zelda that made her rebel and travel to America with her children, rather than live in the sheltered shtetl of Poland. It was her independent nature that saved her from Hitler's ovens, while the majority of our extended family fell victim to them.

As a small child Ben seemed to be gifted, independent, and bookish. In my pushiness of those days, I tried to make him read at three. He did by four—although he rebelled at spelling; English orthography is not logical, so he always spelled words phonetically. He was outstanding in high school chemistry, biology, and physics; won a *Boston Globe* award with his very first oil painting; and could grasp any situation immediately.

As a young teenager he was interested in astrology and discovered classes by the well-known teacher Isabel Hickey, who promoted him to the advanced class. He was wise beyond his years, but always kept to himself. When his pet hamster was mauled by the family cat, he chose to deal with his emotions privately and sort them out by himself before he talked about them.

His mind was quick, logical, and thorough. A lover of mountains, Ben at twelve influenced the whole family to ski, so we all went to Killington, Vermont, to learn the Killington method, which entails the use of skis of graduated length as you progress. (I came to love skiing too: Coasting down the slopes felt almost like a form of worship to me, and I fantasized some kind of Jewish Sabbath service on skis.) Ben studied every ski trail and every car route. His father remembers stopping to rest at a ski trail crossroad, when another skier approached, looking lost and asking for directions. Our son, with characteristic thoroughness, explained every trail and every option. The skier asked his age and marveled at his intelligence. I, however, didn't believe that Ben had the routes so well memorized and argued with him about them. He turned out to be right. Perhaps these kinds of misunderstandings, a result of my own attachment to some fictional image of Ben, drove him more and more into an interior world, far from me. I certainly did blame myself for any behavior that worried me.

When Ben was thirteen, Rabbi Zalman Schachter-Shalomi, the founder of Aleph, the New Jewish Alliance—a post-denominational New Age movement—presided over his bar mitzvah at Congregation Beth El in Sudbury, along with Rabbi Lawrence Kushner before the publication of his many neo-mystical books. In his speech, Ben analyzed Abraham's attempt to sacrifice his beloved son, Isaac, by Divine request, despite the promise of future descendants as numerous as the star in the sky. Looking back on it now, I see a Buddhist sensibility already present in Ben's reasoning. To him there was no real dilemma or contradiction. "The Holy One," he said, "wanted Abraham to be present in the here and now, because the future can only happen if we are present in the here and now. The moment that Abraham was present, the Holy One rescinded the command to sacrifice Abraham's son." The entire congregation of 150 gave Ben a standing ovation. As his face shone in response, I envisioned him as a great rabbinical thinker. That, however, was not to be his chosen path.

It was Ben's love of mountains that first drew him to the Himalayas. He chose to spend his junior year abroad in Nepal, where he became attracted to the warm and friendly people and their mountain culture. As a student of international development, he did a project on the development of tourism in the Everest region (a Buddhist region of what is primarily a Hindu country). After his graduation from Reed College in 1983, he returned to Kathmandu, and through intellectual debates with friends his interest in Buddhism was gradually awakened. Eventually he came into the orbit of Chökyi Nyima Rinpoche, a Tibetan teacher of the Nyingma lineage of Vajrayana Buddhism, who was to become his "root guru."

I remember when Ben was a teenager, the whole family had been enchanted by the 1937 movie *Lost Horizon*, with its depiction of the hidden Himalayan utopia known as Shangri-la, representing an ideal state of consciousness and community. We all saw the movie several times. I sometimes blamed this movie, and my husband's interest in exotic panaceas, for Ben's fascination with Nepal and Buddhism, with its promise of enlightenment. That is, when I wasn't blaming myself.

When Ben was growing up, my husband, Sandy, had declared himself an atheist, despite his religious upbringing, and bluntly dismissed my beliefs that our marriage was *beshert*, Yiddish for "meant to be." Someone whom I now call Der Aybishter (Someone Up There) was watching and had planned our marriage. I kept these beliefs to myself while the god of intellectualism supplanted our Jewish G-d and we stationed ourselves at the cutting edge of New Age ideas.

After earning his PH.D. in psychology, Sandy did animal experiments showing that psychological stress in pregnancy resulted in malformed fetuses; and so I was among the first in 1960 to have a baby—our first child, Elizabeth—by natural childbirth. Students from a nursing class even entered my labor room because they were curious why I was not screaming. A year later Ben was also delivered by natural childbirth. In those days we were politically liberal, but Betty Friedan's book *The Feminine Mystique* (1963) was yet to be published, and so I was pleased to have a boy to carry on our tradition and our name. (Today, both my daughters are career women and doing a great job of carrying on the family tradition.)

We moved to Boston when Ben and Elizabeth were five and six, and thus began one of the happiest times of my life. My husband was an academician in the world of ideas, my children were both in school, and I could write. As a college wife, I became a college "drop-in" at Tufts, where I deepened my love of literature. I frequented all the poetry haunts in Boston and followed poets like Anne Sexton from reading to reading. I had my own poetry readings and my poetry buddies.

The unexpected death of my sister in her mid-forties from kidney failure numbed me into shock and sadness. At that time, one of Sandy's favorite students who was staying with us became enraptured with Esalen, the famous retreat center in Big Sur, California, known for its blend of East/West philosophies and experimental psychotherapies. He demonstrated to us what he had learned there, and our living room became transformed into a Gestalt therapy "hot seat" workshop for me, wherein I began to talk to my dead sister about losing her. This student also went to one of my literary parties and regrouped it into a spontaneous encounter session where we all began to speak our "true feelings" to one another. Regretfully, I didn't return to my poetry circles because some participants thought that the spontaneous encounter group was too disruptive. That killed my dream of publishing a slim volume of my poems. Sandy, however, was so impressed that we had to go to Esalen too for a week, to sample the products of the "growth business," in the words of Fritz Perls, founder of Gestalt therapy in America.

One pocket of peace came during a meditation workshop near the end of our stay. Alan Watts led my group through three days of listening to the sounds of nature. It was a space in consciousness that I was not to find again until years later, in my travels with my son. I was returned to feeling once again that there is something spiritual in this universe beyond rational philosophizing.

While I grieved for my sister, my husband was converted to the new religion of encounter groups and the methodology of Fritz Perls. Although I threw myself into this identity for the sake of "togetherness," I never really felt comfortable in this environment and reacted by retreating into silence or indulging in chatty behavior that caused one psychologist to comment, "Rosie, stop auditioning; you've already got the part!" Although I was disturbed by these new experiences, stronger than that was my need to please others, especially my husband. I did not understand then how to have a separate identity in his presence; instead I fell into a pattern of blame and shame.

Further family losses added to my stress, and my memory of these events is still blurred. Seven months after our return from Esalen, my diabetic brother, upset and pressured by my mother's wild grief, one day poured himself a hot bath, hoping to relax, but it was blistering hot. Since he could not feel sensations in his legs, by the time he realized how intense the heat was, he had developed third-degree burns. Amputations and diabetic coma followed, leading to a torturous death. Now both my siblings, older than me by over a decade, were gone. They had been like parents to me, a buffer against immigrant parents still bewildered by American ways.

In 1970 Sandy and I were delighted by the arrival of our third child, Rebecca. However, as time passed, I realized that I had reproduced my family of origin: first an older daughter, then a son, and then, ten years later, a younger daughter. I became increasingly haunted by the fear that I would experience the same tragedies as in my first family, that there was some strange replication of loss awaiting me. The loss was, of course, my close relationship with my family, which *was* a death to me. Increasingly I found it hard to deal with my family responsibilities in the midst of my grief. Worse yet, I feared that as I approached my mid-forties, the age of my siblings' deaths, I would contract some illness like them and pass away.

My distress deepened when my heartbroken seventy-seven-year-old father succumbed to a stroke. I remember entering the cemetery and thinking that my three-month-old baby was weeping and that I had to cradle her in my arms. As I was throwing the first shovelful of soil on my father's coffin (part of the familial Jewish burial service), I realized that it was I who was crying. When I heard the thud of dirt on the pine box, it startled me like a drum-roll to sorrow, and I began to wail uncontrollably. The sound of my choking sobs called to my mother in the midst of her own numbing grief, and she turned to hold me tenderly and whisper in my ear, "Rokheleh," the Yiddish diminutive of my Jewish name, Rachel. Her voice was like a lullaby that quieted me into silent crying.

In two years, I had lost most of my nuclear family and was responsible for a despondent elderly mother. In years to come, when I began to practice Judaism more ardently, I often thought that, had I performed the traditional mourning period with the usual synagogue support, I would have avoided the despondency that followed. However, the cure then was to participate in more groups and more New Age methodology. Once, I participated in a day-long meditation retreat with speeded-up techniques, using mandalas, bells, and accelerated breathing. By the end of the day, I had lapsed into a trancelike space where I experienced a succession of strange perceptions. I saw no color in the mandala and couldn't get the sound of the bell out of my head for weeks. I called Reb Zalman, who said that I had encountered "the Void." Fear grew in me daily to be in such uncharted territory. I went to the Paramahansa Yogananda retreat in California in a fruitless search for a meditation teacher, while at the same time blaming my husband for the problems caused by all these New Age solutions. We did not have a peaceful family life; it was full of disagreements and interference from outsiders.

During this time of distress I probably did what many Jewish mothers do: turned to my son for emotional support instead of my husband. Ben was a good listener, but playing that role was not good for him. I gradually withdrew from even these confidences and entered a vast loneliness.

Finally I consulted a conventional psychiatrist, who patiently helped me to weed out the frenzy from the facts and brought me back to life. I rented a room in a nearby boarding house that I used as a writing studio; I worked full time, became increasingly religious, attended synagogue services regularly, and talked about these events in varying depth with each family member. I credit my full participation in my Jewish heritage as the most healing influence. Slowly my family life and marriage were healing. As I became more comfortable again in my own skin, I could get closer to my husband, family, and friends. I was proud of my daughter Elizabeth, who had survived the family turmoil and flowered as an artist in her chosen field of photography, married, and had children.

The eighties were years of psychological repair and the pursuit of a corporate career along with an identity as a writer and poet. I was pleased to see my work published in newspapers, anthologies, and prayerbooks; to me, poems *are* prayers, and my writing had become a vehicle for my spiritual healing. My husband entered psychoanalysis with a fine psychiatrist, and this ongoing process effected a great change in him. After the death of his father—a deeply religious man—Sandy's observance of the Jewish year of mourning and prayers allowed a profoundly serious belief in G-d to emerge. He favored the traditional prayer service, all in Hebrew with no English. With this influence, I became even more observant in my own practice, and our marriage dialogue deepened.

After a decade the corporation downsized, and I was laid off. Six months earlier my mother had died, creating a great sadness in my life again. This time, observing the proper Jewish mourning rituals and the solace of friends and congregants allowed me to process my memories and regrets. I was thankful that I had at least managed to say good-bye to my mother as I held her in my arms during her coma and sang the Yiddish lullabies that she had once sung to me. Saying the Kaddish, a mourners' prayer that affirms life, was uplifting. Had I known to do this earlier in my life, I might never have faltered.

Even so, the death of my mother and the loss of my identity as a career woman brought some unavoidable suffering. I read a lot and watched more television than I ever had in my life, but only stories with happy endings. By now, psychotherapy had become spiritually bankrupt for me. I needed a path that would help me ascend out of myself, to make contact with a new potential. Once again I pursued my Jewish spiritual path in earnest. Rebecca was now living in Israel and invited me there. She often remarked that the devout practice of *shiva* observed after her grandfather's death had sparked her to become Orthodox and seek a life of service, and she had found a career in an educational agency in Jerusalem. Finally I made my first pilgrimage to the Holy Land, where Rebecca guided me to the holy places and the tombs of the matriarchs, patriarchs, and rabbinical sages. Upon my return, I recommitted myself to study, writing, prayer, and education in my own Jewish roots; I taught children, created workshops, and became involved with professional Jewish educators' networks. Like Rebecca, I was to learn that coming out of oneself by serving others is in fact a healing service to oneself.

My marriage was finally at peace. By luck and perseverance, my husband and I came back together in a new way after all the storms of my life. The empty nest fostered this and was a return to the first days of our relationship together. In spite of all this progress, I continued to feel remorseful and fearful that my children had been wounded. I saw Ben's entry into Buddhism as a withdrawal in search of calm. I understood it, but I felt like a failure as his mother. I was sure my psychological and spiritual failings had scarred him for life. I felt hurt that he would turn away from my own, dearly beloved tradition. And I feared that in doing so, he had embarked on the path of "idol worship" that is so strongly prohibited in Judaism.

Ben first vowed formally to "take refuge" in the Buddha, the Dharma, and the Sangha in the spring of 1984—an event that I was unaware of at the time. Ironically, this was six months before the publication of my article with the Jewish mother joke. Later he explained that "Buddha" does not mean a particular man, but the potential for enlightenment that exists in everyone; Dharma (the Buddha's teachings) is the path to get there; and Sangha (the community) is the group that supports those who undertake the journey. He assured me that these vows did not mean that he had renounced his Jewishness—that Buddhism allowed you to hold "dual citizenship" in both religions. But at the time, I was not able to hear this.

With this act of refuge, Ben had begun a path that would include many retreats and teachings with prominent Asian teachers. I used to weep when I realized that he would never come home the same again. However, I knew that asking him to finally come home, like the Jewish mother in the joke, would not work. As it turned out, I was asked by him to travel to Europe and Asia to meet his gurus, to experience Buddhist meditation for myself, and to learn more about his chosen way of life.

Buddhist devotees along the way mistook my journey for a pilgrimage to Buddhism. It would require a tremendous leap of faith for me to integrate Buddhism with my Jewish heritage, which had become a tree of life to me, holding my body and soul together through the joys and crises of life. My journey was in fact a pilgrimage to my own son's heart, to try to fathom it. In the process, though, I came to understand myself and what I needed in a way that I would have previously found unfathomable.

2

Tibet on the Hudson

I REMEMBER THE FIRST TIME I HEARD THE REPETITIVE intonations of Tibetan chanting, I was in my dining room in the late eighties. The vowel sounds that growled up from the depths of the chanters' diaphragms startled me into fantasies of communicating with our animal soul. My son's droning addition to the chorus was so deep-voiced that it caused me to look at him with new eyes. The participants included Ben, the lama, and one attendant. My husband and I were the audience to this unexpected concert in our home.

Ben had cooked a lamb roast for his visiting Tibetan teacher, Lama Norlha, on newly purchased kitchenware, which was now designated to be used only for such visiting dignitaries. I already had at least two sets of dishes and pots, as required by *kashrut*, the Jewish dietary laws; now I worried about where to store this third set necessary to meet a new set of rules—the rules for guru kashrut!

The foreign sound issuing from my dining room—a ritual of offering (*puja*) preceding the meal—frightened me so much that I stayed in the kitchen, tearfully wringing my hands and praying, until it was over. I told myself that what they were doing was simply the equivalent of the Hebrew blessings before the meals, yet I was afraid that my son had lost his Jewish soul in some mysterious, exotic sect, as my consultation with an Israeli rabbi indicated. In acceding to my son's wish to offer hospitality to his teacher, had I allowed some pagan blessings to be uttered in my own home? Buddhism, I was told, is not a religion, since Buddhists do not believe in a supreme deity or "self." Who or what, then, were they praying to? As the sounds of puja were repeated at a faster and faster rate, they seemed to be boring a hole into my already wounded heart.

The next time I heard the chanting, it was on Mother's Day 1991, and I was seated next to Lama Norlha in the dining room of his Dharma center, Kagyü Thubten Chöling (KTC), overlooking the Hudson River in Wappinger Falls, New York. Ben had just announced that to deepen his meditation practice, he would be entering a three-year retreat at KTC with Lama Norlha. This was at the suggestion of Chökyi Nyima Rinpoche, who considered Ben one of his best students; the retreat would groom him to be a "junior lama" and have a more senior function in the Rinpoche's entourage. My husband applauded Ben's decision, and it was no secret that if he were younger, this was an adventure that he would have undertaken himself.

I was stunned. *Three years?* Ben would not be able to leave the compound for three years! Worse yet, I would not be allowed to see him. How would he look in three years? Gaunt and hollow-eyed? Would his auburn hair darken even more? More important, what would happen to his Judaism? I feared that he would be lost to me, his mother, forever. For the duration of the retreat he would be following special vows, such as celibacy, and most of the time he would be "staring at a wall" in meditation. Wasn't this some strange form of self-hypnosis or brainwashing? And after the three years, would my Jewish boy become a monk? Oy vey, I would never have descendants, as many as were promised Abraham, to bear the family name!

Here there was no escape from the sounds of the Buddhist ritual. Frightened, I took my shawl, used it as a prayer tent, and, after finding my traveling prayerbook, began to pray next to a nearby window. The resident nuns and monks, some of whom I fantasized were estranged from their American families, found my actions interesting and spiritual. Ben was embarrassed.

Later I walked outside alone through a newly cleared field and then around the fence of his retreat house in the back woods after he had waved farewell. High above the Hudson River, I sang the Shema, the Jewish signature prayer proclaiming One G-d, as I listened again to those rhythmic sounds of puja growling out from the cracks in the wall. Maybe, I thought, I could fold a paper note, like the prayers that people tuck into cracks in the Western Wall in Jerusalem, to communicate with Ben in a meaningful way. This note would be as pleading as any supplication that a Jew could bring to the holy site in Israel. I prayed that he would not forget me or what his Jewish lineage represented.

During the next three years we corresponded, and Ben supplied me with tapes of lectures to keep me informed. Whenever I listened to the tapes, I became anxious, thinking that our tradition was slipping further and further away from Ben. I remembered that he had written his senior thesis on the consequences of the Holocaust, and that he had read many books on Judaism, the Kabbalah, and Jewish mysticism in college and during his stay in Nepal. I prayed that he still retained that interest. While he was gone, I continually scanned the Jewish books left behind on the bookshelf in his room: Eli Wiesel's *Night*, Martin Buber's two-volume *Tales of the Hasidim*, Philip Berg's *Kabbalah for the Layman*, modern Jewish history books by Howard Sachar, Robert Chasan, and Marc Lee Raphael. But it was the underlined passage in Buber's *On Judaism* that raised me up: "The believing Jew (and the believing Jew was the whole Jew) found his unity in his G-d."

My heart beat with the hope that Ben's interest in Judaism would be reawakened during his retreat, even though he had little contact with it. His was one of the most brilliant minds I had ever encountered, and at the same time that I worried that he was involved in a cult, I began to imagine him proudly as the world's expert in both religions. Ben himself never saw any conflict between the two paths, but I could not understand this at the time. Once on a birthday card to me, he wrote, "Mother, will you hold my hand in the dance of the Torah?" I wept in gratitude for days.

He also sent a poem that he'd written for me, called "My Mother Is a Poet." Even today my heart opens when I read it, because he seemed to understand me so well. In it he recalled my researching a local woman abolitionist, Lydia Maria Child, for an article, showing that he understood my feelings of identifying with the underdog. The poem reflected his sympathy with my identity as a poet and a parent, and affirmed my deepest value as a Jew: that living a good life is the essence of seeking wisdom. He urged:

> Mother, if you want to write a book of poems
> Then write in the Book of Life,
> Make it full of mitzvahs.

> Many a great mitzvah is done in silence,
> A smile to soothe a heart of sorrow,
> A Grandmother holding her grandson.

> Mother, in my dreams I have visited Heaven.
> The angels all crowd around to read your book,
> A book of life.
> It's a best seller.

Three years later, in 1994, the long cloister was finally over, and once again I heard the chanting puja-drone prayer as I waited on the hillside of KTC for Ben to emerge from his retreat. I was so thankful to be able to be reunited with him. Impatient to see Ben, I paced up and down the hillside, crunching the fall leaves underfoot. I turned to stride quickly toward the fence around his retreat house, the same house that I had circled with prayers at my last visit there. On my left I could see the Hudson River again through the sparse foliage; on my right at the top of the hill stood my family: my husband, the therapist, with his hair grown whiter, and my elder daughter with her husband and two children; directly before me, my younger daughter, now even more Orthodox in her Judaism, walking toward me with her hands outstretched and compassion in her eyes. On this Friday after Thanksgiving, the Rosenzweigs were the only intact nuclear family waiting for the retreatants among the audience of single parents, friends, and devotees. Amazed, I wondered how my family had come together in this functional, friendly, and supportive manner after years of psychological and spiritual turmoil.

Suddenly, I recognized the sounds rolling out of the back woods. My body snapped to alertness at the chants of puja accompanied by the flat bleating of long, thin horns and the slow palm-slap of drums. The procession snaked out from the bottom of the wooded path. I was silent as I gaped at my only son. Though not stout for his five feet eight inches, Ben—or Karma Sherab Gyurmey, as he was now named (meaning Eternal Wisdom)—had gained some weight. He walked slowly between three monks, followed by six nuns; Lama Norlha led the parade. As they chanted in unison with the drums and horns, I wondered if this was the Tibetan equivalent of the chanting procession of Jews on the Sabbath, singing verses from the Torah and Psalms, marching around the synagogue carrying the Torah scroll just before its reading. Each of the ten retreatants wore maroon robes like the Dalai Lama's and a tall, triangular red hat with gold trim on top.

I hadn't expected the hat.

Some wisps of Ben's auburn hair peeked out from each side; it did seem a little darker than three years ago. Rebecca, standing beside me now, put her arms around me, hugged me, then took my hand and led me up the hill behind the parade. We entered the main house, parked our shoes, and climbed the stairs to the shrine room, with mustard-colored walls hand-painted with white and maroon lotus flowers. A twenty-foot golden Buddha, as tall as the ceiling, presided over a display containing hundreds of small golden Buddhas, blessing us with his hands. So here we were, my

Jewish family among the idols. My idolization of my son had indeed been smashed; the family name might be carried on, but not its Judaism. Idols need not be made of wood and plaster or shaped into human or animal form; they could be dreams, another form of false attachment to images.

The Asian and American congregation included KTC residents in their robes, guests in Tibetan dress or casual L. L. Bean garb, and a few well-behaved children. We all held kataks, white silk scarves to be presented to the Lama as a sign of respect. Ben had prepared them for us and instructed us about their use. As I walked toward Lama Norlha with a dozen kataks, he smiled, took one scarf with both hands, yoked it around my head and neck, and blessed me in Tibetan with a puja melody; I gave the others to my family. There seemed no harm in this simple courtesy of greeting, I rationalized. He chuckled broadly at me, and I remembered his words when he once introduced me to a visiting Tibetan teacher: "Here is Ben's mother. She always sends food." In lieu of chicken soup, I regularly sent Ben my whole wheat and honey banana breads, but I was instructed to send one loaf to the women's retreat, one loaf to the men's retreat (which Ben got to share) and one loaf to Lama Norlha himself. He seemed to like it.

My eyes got wet and then wide and then wet again as I couldn't stop looking at Ben during the formal puja that followed with horns, drums, and gongs. Ben himself was beating the largest gong in sync with the rise and fall of Tibetan chants, first slowly, then in accelerated tempo. I whispered to myself the Hebrew blessing said upon seeing someone after a long absence: *Baruch Atah Adoshem Elohenu Melekh ha-Olam mechayeh ha-metim* (Blessed be You, our G-d, King of the Universe, Who brings life to the dead). Across the room my son-in-law had one arm around each grandson; two rows in front of me were my two daughters. At my side against the window was my husband, looking calm.

Afterward, the retreatants' families and the benefactors sat at Lama Norlha's table with a view of the river. I recognized among the Buddhist followers a charismatic, intellectually brilliant poet who, twenty years ago when I knew him, was quite obese. Now, trimmed of his "lies," as he called them, he was gaunt and white-haired. Obviously a devotee, he had learned to be quite obse-quious to Lama Norlha, a simple man with street-smart wisdom acquired during his exile from his Tibetan homeland. My poet friend wore his change well, and I was amazed and happy for his transformation. It was he who explained the puja rite of after-meal chanting and offering bread to feed the many children of a fierce female mother deity. She would only follow Buddha after he promised that his Sangha would feed these "hungry ghosts." I could certainly relate to this motherly instinct—even in a de-moness.

That night Ben could not join the family in the motel for our observance of the Sabbath, because he had to lead services at KTC. We improvised a long dinner table from the coffee tables in our adjoining rooms and used a sheet for a tablecloth and a water-glass as a vase for flowers. I used my traveling Sabbath candle-sticks and blessed the Sabbath light over two lonely flames. We ate leftover Thanksgiving turkey in challah sandwiches and drank hot tea from my traveling electric urn. As we sat on pillows on the floor, I knew that we were making family memories. Playing with my grandsons on the rug, I missed Ben during our usual Sabbath blessing of the children. Just as I had blessed him in absentia every Friday for the past three years, I uttered the traditional words that reminded us of Joseph's two sons, who kept the faith despite growing up in Pharaoh's court:

> May God make you like Ephraim and Manasseh.
> May the Lord bless you and protect you.
> May the Lord shine His countenance upon you
>   and be gracious to you,
> May the Lord favor you and grant you peace.

Sunday included a round of parties celebrating the completion of the retreat. First we drove to the log cabin home of a neighbor-ing artist, where we heard more chanting, drums, and horns, fol-lowed by a large lunch including piles of Tibetan dumplings. I noticed that the hostess wore a *chuba*, the long wool jumper, silk blouse, and striped apron of the Tibetan mother. Ben had brought one home for me from Nepal, but I could never quite figure out how to wear it. The silk blouse kept riding up and exposing me; with my long strides, my legs kept getting caught in the long skirt; the striped apron finally ripped and fell off. I did, however, wear the jumper backwards like a warm blanket with armholes to ward off the chill of New England winters in front of a roaring fire.

After this hospitality we drove to Karma Triyana Dharma-chakra, the Dharma center in Woodstock, for another reception and ceremony. The building was immense and the shrine room much taller, larger, and more golden than the one in Wappinger Falls; here the sounds of chanting and instruments resonated through the ceiling and echoed toward a forty-foot Buddha. A Westerner, one of the many Jewish Buddhists there, served me the ritual sweet rice with raisins and tea. "Don't worry," he said with a wink, "it's kosher."

A quick tour of the mansion revealed upstairs rooms with rich mahogany furniture and paneling, Oriental rugs, oak floors, and spanking-new equipment, from sewing machines to computers. Downstairs an elderly resident seamstress and housemother kept bowing to me. Mothers of retreatants are quite honored in this tradition.

On the way home, Ben, now dressed in his usual corduroy pants and plaid shirt like his father, began to talk about returning to his beloved Nepal to consult with his "root guru." He also reported how everyone at both Dharma centers, and at lunch in the private home, spoke highly of my friendliness and openness. Maybe I hadn't screwed up so badly after all. Maybe my son even liked me! Maybe he really, really liked me after all!

That evening Ben began talking seriously about my traveling with him to Nepal to meet his guru—an idea he had first broached in letters written from his retreat. He was full of suggestions for the itinerary. On the way to Nepal, he suggested, we could go to southwestern France for a short meditation retreat with Thich

Nhat Hanh, the Vietnamese Zen teacher whose books and tapes Ben kept sending me to help me understand Buddhist principles. Ben thought that this teacher's gentle approach would be a healthy introduction to Buddhism for me.

Ben knew that I would be worried about finding kosher food on our trip, so he assured me that Plum Village was strictly vegetarian. Jewish dietary laws dictate that if one eats meat, the animal must be killed in a prescribed humanitarian way by a licensed Jewish ritual butcher, and that one must not mix meat and dairy products, after the compassionate biblical injunction against "boiling a kid in its mother's milk" (Exodus 23:19). If we ate in restaurants, I would just carefully select vegetarian items, according to my usual custom.

Ben wanted his father to come along on the trip too, but Sandy is not fond of traveling, especially through time zones. His preference for a daily vacation is to walk through the neighboring fields and trails bordering our town and then meditate near some body of water. I, on the other hand, am driven by a natural attraction to new experiences—so long as they don't threaten me. The idea of traveling to Nepal put me in a double bind: it appealed to my intellectual curiosity, but it also made me anxious to think of sojourning in a land of idols and nonkosher meals. On my own I would have never traveled to the third world, where I imagined myself helplessly encountering the outstretched hands of beggars. Their poverty, I feared, would break my heart. Yet I knew I would never have an opportunity like this again to understand my son.

I had been to Europe once before, to accompany my husband to a conference in Munich. Germany made us feel uncomfortable, but it became a pilgrimage of sorts when we paid a wordless, anguished visit to Dachau, for a silent vigil of prayer. Then we enjoyed Vienna and an Austrian spa. I could see nothing as satisfying ahead in this trip, except for the psychological and spiritual work of seeking some bit of wisdom, a platform on which to build the rest of our lives.

I thought of my mother, who lived under the depressive pall of the death of more than eighty relatives in the Holocaust. She had become so phobic about any contact with non-Jews. I wondered what would she have said about these events, this upcoming trip. Whenever my actions would cause her to worry, she used to warn me in a heavy Yiddish accent, "Oy vey, just wait until you have children of your own! You'll see how a mother suffers!"

She was right, I did suffer. Nevertheless, I would try to follow Ben's bar mitzvah advice: to be in the here and now to make our future possible. On this day I would have preferred to be celebrating Ben's rabbinical ordination. But he cared about his Buddhist way of life, and I felt driven, by my caring for him, to integrate it so that I could live with it. Perhaps Ben himself realized that he could never reach enlightenment so long as we were so distant.

3

In the Parisian Jewish Quarter

WE HAD ENTERED THIS BOOKSHOP ON THE RUE DE Rosier, in the Jewish Quarter of Paris—our stopover on the way to Plum Village—because I wanted to see what books European Jews read. Recalling my work in book production at a major corporation, I caressed the fabric covers of several prominently displayed French books on Jewish *mysticisme*. The Holocaust had virtually wiped out an entire world of Jewish culture and scholarship—including the mystical schools of Hasidism—yet here, apparently, was evidence of a thriving fascination with the Jewish mystical tradition.

Next I picked up an English-language book, *The Polish Jewry: History and Culture*, and there was nothing mystical about the sob that forced its sound out of my lips. The large, illustrated book had drawn me like a magnet: my family, the dead ones whom I never met and the living ones who carried death in their memories, came from Poland. I was trying to scan it quickly without being noticed. This book evoked for me a cascade of associations, not only about my family history but also about my studies of Hasidism. This popular movement—founded in seventeenth-century Poland by the Baal Shem Tov ("Master of the Good Name"), who made the esoteric teachings of Kabbalah accessible to ordinary people—emphasizes the ecstatic worship of G-d in everyday life. The Holocaust had killed off most of the great leaders of this joyful movement, and the book painfully reminded me of a time when the Holy One's back appeared to be turned on my people and my family. But I didn't want to have any emotional outbursts when I was near Ben and his expatriate friend Jane, our Jewish Buddhist hostess who had opened her hospitality, her time, and her kitchen to us. Mentioning the Holocaust might touch off an argument between Ben and me, so I didn't want to bring it up.

My tears brought it up instead, and in an instant Jane was at my side as I wept behind a turnaround of picture postcards. One featured the profile of a young Pole with a prominent nose who reminded me of my father, a leatherworker and sometime cantor who used to enchant me as a child, singing "Oyche Choynia" (Dark Eyes) to the mirror while shaving.

Turning back to the book, I showed Jane a photograph of a synagogue like the one that my grandfather had built in Grodno, with his name on the cornerstone. They called it Chorke's Gessel. That synagogue, since burned down, was where my father served as the cantor while my mother sat in the front-row family pew. Suddenly, in memory, I was flashing back to my mother beating her chest at the news of her parents' death, and I recalled how my only living aunt, Fania in Krakow, stunned me with the news in her letter about the more than eighty family members who had perished in Oswiecim. Only later did I find out that *Oswiecim* is the Polish spelling of *Auschwitz*.

Ben was on the other side of the store, but I tried to hide my face from him anyway. He would be very embarrassed by my public reaction. During his retreat we had had an exchange of letters about the Holocaust. He had asked me, pointedly: Why do I, your son, have to be Jewish? I wanted to reply: Why do you, my only son, have to be Buddhist? Although I was trying to refrain from the stereotypical guilt-inducing routines of the Jewish mother, I needed to tell him that we have to be Jewish because of the Holocaust, and I expressed this in heavy emotional terms. I knew, after I had sent the letter, that it would cause him to withdraw from me, but I had to say it. Even though my parents came to North America in the 1920s, settling in Ontario, Canada, the tragic loss of my mother's large, extended family would be felt for generations. I was robbed of grandparents, aunts, uncles, and cousins, and with their loss I was robbed of my personal history. Why be Jewish? Maybe to repopulate the lost Holocaust generation, to keep alive our endangered heritage, to honor the Holy One—and, maybe, to honor my own mother, whose sadness sometimes hung over our house like a cloud of ashes from the chimneys of Auschwitz, to never forget her and the way this tragedy murdered our past.

This book that I showed Jane documented how Spanish Jews flocked to parts of Poland during the Inquisition as if it were a Promised Land—or a Shangri-la. That explained why my grandfather's name was Todros, obviously a Sefardic name, and maybe it explained why Jews have Grecian or Mediterranean noses. While Poland had a crazy-quilt of laws that sometimes discriminated against and sometimes protected Jews, depending on the whim of the locals, it also offered life.

Grodno, the city of my parents' birth, was once a major Jewish learning center, and Poland, which once held the largest population of Jews in the world, was an important center of Jewish mysticism. What meditations, I wondered, were practiced in the land of my parents?

Jane now needed to sit down. She had been in a severe automobile accident and walked with the help of metal canes that clattered with her every step, signaling her discomfort. Despite this, during our one-day stopover, she volunteered to guide us through the labyrinth of the Paris Métro. Noticing the homeless sleeping in the subway, she continually described Paris as a compassionate city that allowed these unfortunates to spend the night in heated stations during the cold winter. She now became the embodiment of Buddhist compassion as she tried to understand my emotional reactions to the book on Polish Jewry.

As I spoke to her, I stroked the book, wanting to buy it. I told her the story that I taught my young students in Hebrew school before I left: Once a German Holocaust guard forced his Jewish prisoners to sew a shirt from a Torah scroll for him to wear so that they would be forced to honor him. The inmates, knowing his ignorance of Hebrew, chose the parchment page containing curses inflicted on the wicked. While the inmates were forced to parade around the guard who was dressed in these curses, another guard approached. Mistaking his fellow Nazi for a raucous Jew, the second guard killed the first. Here was an example of the Buddhist doctrine of karma, as well as the biblical principle that we reap what we sow.

By now Ben had found his way to us. I expressed my wish to buy the book in my hands, but as the financially responsible party on our trip, he advised against such an expensive purchase so early in the journey. So instead, I selected some postcards, one of my father's lookalike and another of a Polish synagogue where I imagined my father having sung. We crossed the street to the kosher bakery, where we bought a challah for the Sabbath meal we would have the next night at Plum Village, the meditation community of Thich Nhat Hanh.

En route to the subway, I noticed a synagogue and hesitated in front of it. Whenever I travel, I always search out local synagogues to say a few prayers, to learn about the locale from people who live there, and to feel less like a stranger in a strange land. Now, with my two young companions, I held myself back as I watched a man exit from one of the doors. His beard, dark hat, and suit told me that this was an Orthodox synagogue and that the other entrance was designated for me, because men and women sit separately. I began to find many reasons for not entering: that I was improperly dressed, that Ben would have to sit separately, and that Jane might feel uncomfortable. I mentioned a news report of armed guards at the Paris synagogues because of recent threats. Standing with my two Jewish apostates in front of this synagogue, I continued my internal debate about entering. Could I really pray in their presence? Was I frightened? Was I ashamed? Had this journey drawn me away from my heritage? Maybe, I convinced myself, on the way back I would feel freer.

Around the time of Ben's retreat, I had consulted two prominent Israeli rabbis who were visiting the States. Rabbi Eliyahu Alfasi, a disciple of the Sefardic mystic Baba Sali, warned me about Ben's losing his soul in idol worship, the classic fear of Jews. Rabbi Adin Steinsaltz, the great Talmud scholar, explained the Jewish objection to breaking up the Deity into component parts, thus denying the reality of the One Power. With the warnings of both sages echoing in my mind, still I couldn't fathom why I didn't enter that synagogue. Maybe I lacked confidence that I could inspire Ben and Jane to appreciate the experience. Would they feel like voyeurs as I prayed in their presence for their return to Judaism? I felt like a failure, unable to move them or myself.

So we didn't enter the synagogue.

Earlier that day, alone with Ben and his map, we did a quick one-day walking tour of the city. The rivers were high because of heavy rains, so the French memorial to the Holocaust martyrs was underwater and closed to the public. Ben wanted to cross the street to the Notre Dame Cathedral and admired its towering buttresses. A visiting choir had just finished singing in the cavernous sanctuary. I felt strange entering and sitting amid these Christian echoes. Perhaps this was my chance to rehearse, once again, being a stranger in a strange land.

Later that night, at bedtime, Jane and Ben sat in the kitchen to talk while I tried to sleep. They asked me to please sleep with my feet away from the many images of Buddhas in the room. I tried to say the nighttime prayers from my traveling prayerbook, but the sight of Ben's packet of long prayer sheets on the coffee table distracted me. Curiosity compelled me to open it alongside my small prayerbook. If I squinted, the Tibetan and Hebrew characters seemed like calligraphic cousins. Who would translate one to the other for me? As I drifted off to sleep, I wondered what ecumenical dreams might await me, after such an ecumenical day.

4

Go Slowly, Breathe, and Smile

BEN WAS NERVOUSLY PACING THE FLOOR OF THE TRAIN station near Bordeaux, the Gare de Ste Foy la Grande. During the express train ride from Paris to Libourne, and then the slow local one to this country station, *mon cher fils* had carried the heaviest two duffel bags, a book bag, and his backpack. Taught during his retreat to honor and care for his mother, he was very endearing as he took full responsibility for finances and scheduling. He also assumed the responsibility for pacing while waiting for our ride to Thich Nhat Hanh's Plum Village in Meyrac, Loubés-Bernac. With Ben in charge of worrying, my gardening passion pulled me outside to observe the local foliage. The mottled tree trunks surrounding the parking area looked to be sycamores, a species whose leafy canopies graced two of my favorite places: the drive along Boston's Charles River and Bryant Park outside of the New York Public Library. These poor French cousins, however, had been beheaded at thirty feet above the ground and forced to grow their branches horizontally, bumping, braiding, and knotting themselves together. In the summer this contorted topiary formation must provide a cool leafy overhang, but now, in February, its bare bones distressed me. Were these trees mine, I would allow them their natural elegance to grow gracefully into high umbrella curves.

Could I do the same for my son? Could I allow him to naturally choose his own spiritual path without forcing him into the heritage of his ancestors? Or would this journey with him influence *me* to bend and bow as unnaturally as those poor trees over my head? After this journey with my son, what shape would my life take? Now *I* had begun to pace.

The arrival of our driver, a tentative young woman in an oversized L. L. Bean sweater, cut off my gloomy worries. I realized that my usual predisposition to clothe my experience in poetic images and metaphors influenced my thoughts now. I usually deal with painful experiences this way: the act of constantly trying to write a poem helps me deal with discomfort and realize how I'm feeling. While I was combining my Jewish mother's obsessive worrying with my poetic need, I realized that Ben had already engaged the young lady in conversation. Apologizing for making us wait, she drove us through rows and rows of grape vineyards. In a few months they would leaf into color, but now each staked thick vine trunk was cut back to one single dark and hardy branch; here pruning results in a more productive harvest. Each stump reminded me of my new metaphor as we passed the farmers' trailers full of small, carefully cut logs for their stove, the central heat of the winter.

The sign on the long driveway to the Village des Pruniers (Plum Village) read: ALLEZ DOUCEMENT, RESPIREZ ET SOURIEZ. This was the last French that I would see for the duration of my ten-day visit; while I was there, mostly English and Vietnamese are spoken on these farms with their 1,250 plum trees. The sign's advice—"Go slowly, breathe, and smile"—evoked the type of Buddhism practiced here under the guidance of Thich Nhat Hanh (known as Thây): resident Zen master, poet, and peace activist nominated by Martin Luther King, Jr., for the Nobel Prize, and founder of a Buddhist university, the Vietnamese School of Youth for Social Service, and the Order of Interbeing, whose historic contributions were one on the building stones of the movement called "engaged Buddhism."

Thây's dictum is not the "I think, therefore I am" of Descartes, but rather "I think, therefore I am not." His teaching is in the Zen tradition of Buddhism, *zen* being the Japanese pronunciation of the Chinese *ch'an*, transliterated from the Sanskrit *dhyana*, all of which mean "meditation"; the Vietnamese term for Zen is *thien*. The Vietnamese Buddhist tradition might be considered a unique marriage of Zen with the *vipassana* tradition from Thailand. *Vipassana* means insight, which is not just an intellectual exercise but arises out of the calm stability of the mind trained by concentration. Thây teaches mindfulness, grounded in the awareness of breathing and applied to all the daily tasks and relationships of life, especially the healing of difficult psychological states.

Ben unloaded his luggage in the Upper Hamlet, a separate collection of buildings that housed the men, monks, residents, and visitors. Each hamlet had its own separate kitchen, dining facilities, meditation hall, and schedule. I learned that I could only see my son at appointed times, and I felt a little pang at not being able to share the daily routine with him. (Actually the next day, on that first Friday evening—the beginning of the Jewish Sabbath—I got him to join me for dinner, and the nuns in the kitchen complained; I guess they estimate the quantities of food pretty accurately.) He immediately found a friend for tea and conversation by the time I departed with our driver for the Lower Hamlet. Passing through the heart of this valley of vineyards where a mirrored pond dramatically reflected the cloudless sky, I remembered the Shangri-la of *Lost Horizon*. The idyllic, peaceful feeling of these rolling hills in this countryside triggered memories of the expansive landscape of the movie, with its dome of blue sky.

Arriving at the Lower Hamlet for women, families, and couples, I was greeted by Helga, a blond German woman who brought me tea along with her introductions to registration and the housekeeping systems; I enjoyed the warmth of her company. After a tour of the grounds and buildings, I found my sparsely fur-

nished room on the second floor of a barn equipped with one bare
bulb, two mattresses on the floor, and a newly plumbed bathroom
downstairs for the entire dormitory. The hallway, stairs, and walls
smelled of new wood, recently installed. These modernized stone
buildings, built at least a hundred years ago, pleasantly surprised
me. I had expected outhouses and mud huts. I left my pack on the
floor of my room and found my way back to the main buildings.

Soon afterward, Sister Eleni, a cheerful American with a shaved
head and long gray nun's dress, found me; she was to be my main
guide and advisor. Her gentle eyes seemed weary yet strong. She
constantly demonstrated Thây's teachings on the benefits of smiling, which, he says, brings peace and happiness to both ourselves
and others. "The source of a true smile is an awakened mind," he
says, and the practice of smiling nourishes this awareness. This
teaching reminded me of the Hasidic notion of acting in a holy
way even though we might not feel like it: eventually, if we keep
doing good deeds (*mitzvot*) or acting as if we believe, we influence
our consciousness to sincerely embrace the holy life. It could be
thought of as a Jewish parallel to Buddhist "mind training."

Eleni asked me whether I'd had any previous experience with
meditation and Buddhism. I told her how I had first been taught
at Esalen by Alan Watts, whose course introduced a new calmness
to me after the painful loss of my sister, brother, and father. Afterward, during a dark time of intense pain in the seventies, I had
attended a month-long retreat in meditation yoga-style at the Self-
Realization Fellowship in California. In the eighties, I had visited
several Buddhist teachers. For example, Ben took Sandy and me
to Karma Triyana Dharmachakra, a center of the Kagyü lineage
of Tibetan Buddhism in Woodstock, New York, where we heard
the teachings of the third Jamgon Kongtrul. I also took a class in
Insight Meditation with Larry Rosenberg—one of the many Jews
who have become teachers of Buddhism in our country. It included walking meditation, which I found to be a useful tool
for the acceptance and ultimate transformation of strong and
painful emotions. In this variation of mindfulness meditation, one
walks very slowly, alone or in a group, with awareness of breath-

ing and of each step taken. Whereas it was hard to sit in meditation during a period of struggling with painful feelings, the act of
walking seemed to lessen their intensity. I used to call this practice
"the walking cure," as opposed to Freud's "talking cure"; it
seemed to acknowledge that painful memories reside in the body
and that some form of physical movement allows them to work
themselves out nonverbally. The famous Hasidic master Rabbi
Nachman of Breslov used to recommend long walks as an anti-
dote to depression.

I did not tell Sister Eleni that during my participation in various
Eastern meditation groups, I was always the only erect person in
a roomful of prostrating devotees, because I was unwilling to bow
down in violation of my heritage. Judaism has its own tradition of
bowing: the Israelites bowed full face down in the Tabernacle in
the desert, and later in the Holy Temple in Jerusalem. While modern Jews bow from the waist during certain parts of the daily and
weekly service, for most the only full prostrations occur during
the Yom Kippur supplications. Additionally, there are stories of
Hasidic rabbis assuming this posture for hours in front of the synagogue ark, the repository of the holy Torah scrolls. But for Jews,
it is prohibited to bow before images, idols, statues, or living
human beings who are considered deities.

> Do not have any other gods before Me. Do not represent
> [such gods] by any carved statue or picture of anything
> in the heaven above, on the earth below, or in the water
> below the land. Do not bow down to [such gods] or
> worship them.   (EXODUS 20:3; *Aryeh Kaplan translation*)

We went to the zendo, a large, long sanctuary with two circles
of meditation mats and pillows, a life-size golden Buddha at one
end, and a large potbelly stove at the other. Eleni helped me stack
and shape three pillows into a personal meditation saddle and introduced me to Plum Village's routine of practice. We were to sit
facing the wall with its irregular rounded stones for a half hour;
then the bell would signal the walking meditation clockwise

around the room; then the bell would announce fifteen more minutes of sitting meditation with intermissions for stretching. There was a liberal attitude toward easing one's restlessness throughout. This was certainly less demanding than some of the "no pain, no gain" masters I had encountered in the past. And it was welcome news to me, with my problem knees.

In her soft light voice, Eleni explained Thich Nhat Hanh's bell meditation, in which the sound of a temple bell is used to remind people to bring their attention back to the present moment. Whether they are indoors or out, the sound of the bell invites the members of the community to stop whatever they are doing, saying, or thinking, as if in mid-dance, slowly take three breaths mindfully, and return to their "true self" within before resuming activity or conversation. Later, when I observed people doing this, bowing their heads and putting their palms together, I briefly questioned whether they were unconsciously worshiping the bell like an idol, but I dismissed this before I added even more discomfort to my aversion to idol worship.

Eleni described how a small French bell begins the daily walking meditation after the sitting meditation. A bowl bell calls us to take food from the buffet and signals the beginning of the meal, which is eaten in silence; and this same bell tells diners when they may begin to converse with their neighbors. The prospect of silence was attractive to me, and I looked forward to it as an opportunity to sort out my thoughts and impressions. The large hanging bell outside announces the meal assemblies, the meditation times, the outdoor walking meditation through the roads and fields, and the discussion times; it also rings before bedtime and the beginning of the wordless evening. And, oh yes, the clock chimes every fifteen minutes, and the telephone in the hallway punctuates all activities several times during the day and night.

After explaining all this, Eleni invited me to meditate with her. I had never joined a single partner before, using the common silence to reinforce a silent attention to oneself. After a half hour, we arose, refreshed. She bowed to the Buddha at the conclusion of her meditations and didn't notice that I abstained.

After Sister Eleni had finished with the orientation sessions, she told me to meet with the nun in charge of work assignments, whom I privately dubbed the "work sergeant." Eleni explained these work assignments and the "lazy days" as well as my "jet-lag rest day." She showed me the large white board with the day's schedule and the retreatants' work assignments. She explained how we were to be mindful during our work, not to be too rushed, and simply enjoy the task while we do it. It created some insight for me about how to live in meditation.

Back in the dining room, Eleni broached the idea of my participating in the ceremony of accepting the Five Wonderful Precepts. I remember reading about these principles in the *Plum Village Chanting Book* that Ben had given me, and I had found nothing offensive in them; actually they seemed close to the Noahide laws of Judaism. These are the commandments given to the Gentiles, or "children of Noah," and they relate to idolatry, blasphemy, murder, theft, sexual relations, eating the limb of a living animal, and establishing courts of law. Apparently Thây had rewritten and elaborated the five traditional Buddhist vows concerned with killing, stealing, lying, sexuality, and intoxication, to transform them into positive practices.

The idea of a formal ceremony worried me. It sounded to me like a monastic ordination—or maybe it was a Buddhist bat mitzvah? Whatever it was, I hoped that it did not involve bowing down to Buddha. "Dharma discussions" were scheduled where I would be able to ask these questions, and I was glad to wait for them.

Eleni gave me a text called "Touching the Earth: Five Prostrations." Here it comes, I thought, the head-on collision with the Jewish tradition—specifically the commandment about not bowing down to any graven images. These prostrations pay respect to the ancestors of the blood family, of the spiritual family, of the national family (America, in my case), of all the loved ones, and to reconciliation with those who inflicted personal suffering on us. The ideas were noble, but I couldn't bow to ideas—only to G-d, the Holy One of Blessing.

"My ancestors," I told Eleni, "would have a *conniption* if I bowed down to them!" Too many martyrs in my ancestry had suffered at the hands of Regents, Pharaohs, Hitlers, and Hamans for me to disrespect them with this act. Respectfully I took the texts with me to study. I did not want to insult my hosts, but my conscience was pacing back and forth inside my psyche.

Fortunately our meditation session had calmed me enough to make me sleepy at bedtime. I got lost trying to find my dormitory in the dark, and a tiny Vietnamese grandmother who knew no English led me to the building. Was she one of the boat people whom Thây had saved? I wondered as I groped for my bedroom door. The sound of light sawing greeted me; my roommate was already asleep on her mattress.

After reading quickly through the Five Wonderful Precepts, I lowered myself onto my bed and turned out the light. What Shakespearean brave new world, what vision of Shangri-la, had I entered?

In a wink I was asleep.

5

Plum Village Dreams

A profile of a single, larger-than-life, disembodied human eye was watching from the foreground. At first it seemed like a foreground prop on a stage with a white sky illuminating the landscape. In the middle of the middle ground, a round, dark seed-pod rested on the earth. As the scene took on life, this disembodied eye blinked from time to time, but now it was gazing as if in meditation. The time seemed to be twilight.

A dark human figure in a dark caped coat glided toward it like a cloaked ballet dancer floating on air. The figure entered from stage left diagonally opposite the eye and came like a light breeze. Moving slowly closer, this slender silhouette briefly brushed the pod with a circular motion; this touch ignited a series of internal sparks illuminating an inner pod of light housed within the darker, larger pod. Each spark grew, glowed, and cast its beam of light in all directions, while the dark dancer continued moving.

Behind this landscape moving in a dancelike flow, the moon and stars rose like the backdrop to a stage. The pod, star-specked with peepholes of light, became larger, grew feet, and slowly moved *around with the figure, who now seemed to be a graceful man. All three—the slender man in his caped coat, this large light-seeded pod, and the eye—entered into one continuous contagious movement together; all were one with the dance.*

Then slowly the dancer grazed away from the living seed with its eyebeam-flashlights and passed on out of sight. Briefly I thought that this man might be Thây. All lights unsprouted back into the shrunken, sleeping pod. The large human eye, looking sideways at the whole scene, tall as the scene itself, tall as Thây had been, then closed its lid and rested. The stage was darkened into a larger sleep.

Blinking awake, I stared at the Thursday morning light casting sunbeams through the skylight and groped for my glasses, in the process dislodging a pebble from the stone wall. Thây had vanished from my consciousness and the room.

I puzzled over the prominence of my mind's eye, with its large lid, blue iris, and dark pupil, appearing in the corner of my dream tableau. I closed my eyes and entered that surreal space again. The Jewish sages took a great interest in dreams, calling them "one-sixtieth part prophecy," and many instances of their interpretation are recorded in the Talmud. The tradition accepts that not just prophets and kings but even ordinary individuals may receive divine guidance in their dreams. I wondered what kind of personal prophecy my vision of the night might hold? It did not seem to be an ordinary dream.

This morning I welcomed Plum Village's rule of silence until after breakfast. Silence roused me from my bed, and silence sat with me and walked with me during our morning meditations in the zendo. Silence called me to breakfast with the sweet invitations of bell-ringing. When the bells gave the community permission to speak, I didn't join the soft murmur of conversations amid the clicks and clinks of tableware. My thoughts were still occupied by the dream space of the previous night.

Before the trip I had written Thây from home, and, again upon arrival, requesting a private interview with him. Ben had said that we had a good chance of being granted such an interview, as Thây liked to promote harmony in family life. Helga had given a "wait and see" response to my inquiries. A ridiculous question arose in my thoughts about my dream: could it be that Thây was able to perform a "consciousness scan"? Was he examining the state of my insight to decide whether he should see me?

Embarrassed at this magical thinking, I walked around the dining room in silence and noticed a new treat on the buffet—a container of plum preserves that the nuns were heaping on their porridge. I followed their example. This proved to be the awakening of a ten-day treat indulgence. Food sometimes helps me think better. When I returned to my table, I had decided that dreams simply reflect the dreamer's life situation present at the moment of interpretation.

I remembered how different therapists in my past had taken the same dream and dismembered it according to their particular school of thought, or bias. According to a tape of one of Thây's lectures that Ben had mailed me during his retreat, everyone's mind contains seeds of every kind of feeling, thought, and behavior in a "store-consciousness." The growth of each seed depends upon the nurturing environment. If the seeds of anger are nurtured, then we exhibit angry behavior; if the seeds of love are watered, then we become loving individuals. Thây disagrees with psychotherapists who believe that anger can be expelled by encouraging its expression. As a wounded veteran of the spill-the-guts, punch-the-pillow world of psychobabble groups, I appreciated Thây's questioning that such an exercise helps us to get us in touch with our feelings. "It doesn't even get you in touch with the pillow," he says.

Thây advocates taking care of negative emotions with mindful meditation, understanding them, and transforming them. Mindful breathing calms; calm brings the peace and serenity that restore us; restoration brings insight, and insight brings transformation. As the rotting flower enters the compost heap and becomes transformed through its seed into a flower again, so can anger change into compassion with understanding. Teaching American and European psychotherapists how to use his practice in therapy, Thây offers retreats on Buddhist psychology. He has also done effective work with American Vietnam War veterans on their post-traumatic syndrome symptoms.

As I enjoyed my plum-flavored porridge, I reflected that my dream, whatever it might prophesy, indicated that some seeds of consciousness within me had been stirred. Thây says that the cloud's rains, the sunshine, and the earth are all contained in the growth of the flower. What flowers would grow from my contact with him? What light would be set free within which seeds in my consciousness?

The dining hall bell signaled the cessation of conversation in order to hear announcements, work assignments, and news. Even though I was allowed a "jet-lag" day to rest from work, I wanted to get to my assignment immediately, since I wouldn't be working during the Jewish Sabbath, which would begin the following evening at sundown and last till sundown on Saturday. There are certain classes of work that are not done on Shabbat—the seventh day, on which G-d rested from the Creation—including many common tasks like cooking, washing, writing, and gardening.

I was glad to get a garden greenhouse to tend, because I found that indoor and outdoor cleaning helps me put my thoughts in order. Working in the soil grounds me and brings me to a natural union with the process of creation. The Buddhist notion of rein-carnation as a recycling of energy is understandable to me when I become part of the seasonal cycle of seeding, growth, weeding, and composting. The compost pile is a favorite image of Thây's when he describes how the seed is in the flower, the flower in the seed, how the cloud is in the rain, and the rain in the cloud; the rain and the sun and the seed and the flower are all one in "inter-being." This is Thây's poetic term for the way all things that exist are interconnected. Human beings, too, Thây says, exist in inter-being with every other thing.

Helga's announcement interrupted my thoughts: all Plum Vil-lage residents and visitors were invited to an ordination ceremony for a new nun and monk. After our work meditation, the women drove to the men's hamlet for the event, where I was glad to see Ben. When he showed me his hut and his room, I realized that the women were pampered in luxury. His quarters, with four men to a room, were even more spartan than mine. His bed was a thin padded board on four piles of cinderblocks, and the bathroom was outside. The dining and cooking areas were smaller and more makeshift, but there was also a grove of bamboo, lovely landscaping, and an elegance to the sanctuary. Compared to Asia, I was told, these simple accommodations weren't bad, but the nights were damp and cold. No wonder everyone was always sniffling and dissolving vitamin C salts in hot water. With no hair to warm their heads, and cotton robes as their usual garb, I hoped they all at least had warm socks and good long underwear. Ben and I compared notes until the bell called everyone into the large zendo, with men on one side, women on the other, all seated on the neat rows of meditation pillows. The room was full of many new arrivals from Europe and Asia, including many more Vietnamese families.

This zendo featured a golden Buddha seated before a long Oriental hanging. In the corner of the expansive room against the glass-paned doors, a studied arrangement of tall orchid plants with sprays of small flowers formed a haiku for the eyes, displaying the Asian talent for beauty in sparseness. The local monks and nuns in gray robes sat in the front rows of the center aisle; behind them were Asians and Caucasians in Western dress. There were a hundred of us, in close arrangement on pillows and mats. We became a comfortable cross-legged crowd, sitting calmly knee to knee, elbow to elbow.

Suddenly, the congregation rose when a petite Asian man dressed all in khaki glided in and approached a small table arranged with Buddhist tools of prayer. This was Thây. Neatly stacking his coat and hat, he sat down, straight-backed, to face us, and we resumed our seats. Immediately, the ceremony began with the clonk-tonk of a wooden instrument accompanied by the fine, resonant tones of a rubbed-rim bowl bell. Promises, vows, and a rhythm of chants in English and Vietnamese orchestrated each novice's walk down the center aisle to be married in celibacy to devotion to Buddha, Dharma, and Sangha.

Each walked toward an artfully written sign behind the golden Buddha that read, "Congratulations on your ordination, Feb. 9, '95, Ivar and Kim-Hoa." Ivar, six foot two inches tall, angular and thin, with a craggy face and a long neck, was the first to take his vows. As he bent low to receive the silk shawl of blessing and his certificate, Thây seemed like an elf by comparison. Enveloped in his newly donned gray cotton robes, the new monk stood erect and seemed even taller. The nun seamstress must have taken twice as long to make these. Later I saw Ivar thank her cordially for her efforts.

The novice nun Kim-Hoa was a striking young beauty who held her palms strong and flat against each other. As she stepped shyly and slowly toward Thây, her silky black shoulder-length hair swept gracefully around her face. She stopped tentatively, and the long blue silk *aodai* covering her black silk pants lifted gracefully and came to rest. Smiling, he coaxed her forward, and the whole congregation smiled too—except for one wet-faced older Vietnamese woman standing next to her husband, who was also weeping. This had to be her mother, and my tear ducts opened immediately in sympathy. Once during my own puberty, I naively wished for the peaceful life of a nun, picturing myself calmly writing by a window in a stone tower away from the frenzy of my Polish immigrant family noisily coping with the new world. Now this mother was saying good-bye to grandchildren she would never know. My mother would have unleashed a public hysteria beyond the end of the service.

When Thây left in a hush of standing respect, half the congregation followed him, but I was drawn to this young nun and her family as she was stripped of any signs of vanity. Taking turns, her sister nuns began shaving off her hair. It reminded me of the Orthodox tradition practiced by some Jewish brides, who shave their hair before ritually donning the customary marriage wig. I photographed each dark lock falling and especially the honor of the last lock given to the mother. A stronger, serene beauty, newly robed in gray without the distractions of fashion, emerged with only a brush of black on her scalp. I began to understand the serenity that Ben sought when he took his vows.

Thây's kindness toward the nuns' parents was evident in his next Dharma talk, yet he seemed to be speaking directly to me. He described how the monastic life allows for more freedom from attachment, how meditation leads to freedom, how the freedom affects the devotee's whole family, who has "an ambassador from the Buddha-land" who no doubt will be able to "save the whole family; for if we cannot save our family, then we cannot save other people." The monk or nun has more freedom to be present for the family, and "the family has someone they can take refuge in," someone who has become "the foundation of the family." He said that a letter home from a monk or nun can bring liberation through awakened understanding. Certainly Ben during his retreat had written his grandmother a letter so full of poetic appreciation for this frail eighty-five-year-old widow that she said, "Whatever he's learning in that place, he's doing the right thing." Her husband, during his lifetime, had built up and cared for an orthodox synagogue in Brooklyn.

As the nun's family circled her for some private time, I needed to walk outside. Past the bamboo grove toward a clearing, there on the rise before me, I saw the ageless Thây in his khaki coat and round wool hat, leading a multitude in slow walking meditation. He walked at the same pace as his figure in my dream of the previous night. Now he was surrounded by a rhythm of yellow, orange, and mustard robes slowly moving in the breeze, and framed by his followers with palms prayerfully pressed together. Breathing almost in unison, they walked slowly and precisely with their leader in a unified meditation. Beside him was a big-boned, lean Japanese Zen master in his black robes with a prominent brown padded fabric breastplate and large, long sleeves almost to his knees. He was strong, tall, and muscular, walking with a hard dignity, bearing, and presence next to the slight-figured Thây, this poet in motion who could touch but not disturb, whose breathing led this army of peace gliding over the green unmown pasture, whose energy was and is like a calm conscience throughout the community, here and abroad.

His motion seemed timeless and full of peace, just like the essence of the Sabbath, which has been described as an island in time.

His "peace in every step" reminded me that Shabbat was approaching the very next day. I hoped that I could enter that island in time as gracefully as Thây led this international congregation.

6

To Bow or Not to Bow

THE SCAMPER OF LITTLE PAWS ACROSS MY MATTRESS
startled me into wakefulness. Blinking and wide-eyed, I squinted
into the moonlit darkness and cried out.

My roommate groaned and exclaimed, "Again?"

Apologetic for my outburst, I lay motionless and hoped she
could go back to sleep. A small mouse ran under the radiator beside me with a piece of challah in its mouth! Barely breathing, I finally heard Peggy's sleep buzz again. Now I wished that Ben and
I had eaten the entire bread during last night's private family Sabbath ritual: we lit the candles and blessed, broke, and ate the challah. Now this little rodent, wanting to be part of our challah tradition, reopened the door to the events preceding our Sabbath
ceremony.

Yesterday I had been struggling with Plum Village's invitation
to accept the Five Wonderful Precepts through a formal ceremony. Assured by Peggy's breathing that she was asleep again, I
searched for my bedside flashlight. Propping my copy of Thây's

Five Wonderful Precepts against the challah on my chest, I beamed a light on the first one.

> The First Precept: Aware of the suffering caused by the destruction of life, I vow to cultivate compassion and learn ways to protect the lives of people, animals, plants, and minerals. I am determined not to kill, not to let others kill, and not to condone any act of killing in the world, in my thinking, and in my way of life.

This seemed to correspond to the sixth commandment, "Do not murder." There was no parallel anywhere in these precepts to the first three biblical commandments, which establish faith in one Supreme Deity, because there is no Buddhist vocabulary for the One G-d. The fourth commandment about keeping the Sabbath also had no place here. The fifth commandment about honoring parents had already been addressed by Sister Eleni when she gave me the text on the five prostrations: Buddhists bow daily to their ancestors and parents.

Nothing here disagreed with my personal Jewish theology. Thây's first precept is also a political statement supporting peace as well as vegetarianism. It could even cover preservation of ecology systems. Holy environmentalism! Furthermore, the first precept's acknowledgment of the life in all sentient beings reinforces the Jewish mystical premise that the First Light of G-d is present in all things.

Thây's next precept was more than an extension of the eighth commandment against stealing.

> The Second Precept: Aware of the suffering caused by exploitation, social injustice, stealing, and oppression, I vow to cultivate loving-kindness and learn ways to work for the well-being of people, animals, plants, and minerals. I vow to practice generosity by sharing my time, energy, and material resources with those who are in real need. I am determined not to steal and not to possess

anything that should belong to others. I will respect the property of others, but I will prevent others from profiting from human suffering or the suffering of other species on Earth.

Here was a promise to give to charity. The Hebrew equivalent is *tzedakah,* which in translation is more than charity; it is righteousness. We pledge tzedakah as a tithe on our material profits, as a promise in the name of a dear departed one—as an obligation, not a recommendation. Jews habitually form small tzedakah collectives and vote on the recipients. Every Jewish community promotes charitable donations and philanthropy, and even nonobservant Jews honor this central value of our heritage. For, as Reb Nachman says, "If we do not help a person in trouble, it is as if we caused the trouble."

Thây's precept was compatible with my beliefs and also included environmentalism. It was obvious that alleviation of suffering was an important Buddhist premise.

Today was to be the lay ceremony for accepting the Five Wonderful Precepts, and today I had to decide whether I would participate. I felt that these moral cautions contained nothing disagreeable to me. Ben told me that they were based on the five basic commitments that he had made during his three-year retreat: not to kill, steal, lie, indulge in sexual activity, or use intoxicants. These vows are required of all Buddhist monks, nuns, and ordained lay persons. Thây had made them more inclusive and less rigid for the lay Westerner.

The traditional Buddhist monk's vow of celibacy was modified for laypeople in Thây's third precept; it was now a vow against "sexual misconduct . . . to protect the safety and integrity of individuals, couples, families, and society." It was a vow to abstain from "sexual relations without love and a long-term commitment." This precept seemed like an elaboration of the seventh commandment, against adultery.

The fourth precept, initially against lying, was expanded to "cultivate loving speech." This sounded much like the rabbinical injunction against *lashon ha-ra* (the evil tongue), or gossip. However, Thây had added the promise to cultivate deep listening while others speak. If this practice were to be universally adopted, as his Order of Interbeing hoped, world peace would be a present reality.

Thây's fifth precept, an elaboration of the Buddhist devotee's vow against consuming liquor, was expanded to the pursuit of good physical and mental health and "mindful consumption." It even includes the "ingestion" of sensory impressions:

> I am determined not to use alcohol or any other intoxicant or to ingest foods or other items that contain toxins, such as certain TV programs, magazines, books, films, and conversations. I am aware that to damage my body or my consciousness with these poisons is to betray my ancestors, my parents, my society, and future generations. I will work to transform violence, fear, anger, and confusion in myself and in society by practicing a diet for myself and for society. I understand that a proper diet is crucial for self-transformation and for the transformation of society.

I did believe in Thây's precepts. It was the ceremony that worried me, with its forbidden vows and bows. Even though six hundred thousand of my ancestors had vowed at Mount Sinai to uphold the Ten Commandments, vowing in a Buddhist context seems inappropriate for a Jew, and if construed as worship it would be forbidden just as bowing is. Deuteronomy 23:24 says: "What issues from your lips, you are to keep, and you are to do as you vowed to YHWH your G-d, willingly, as you promised with your mouth." I believe therefore that a vow has G-d as my witness, so to break a vow is to break faith with Divinity. This is why Jews do not take vowing lightly. The Bible obliged a vow-breaker to confess and then make a sacrifice called a guilt-offering. A vow thus has the force of a commandment. I couldn't easily bind myself to these "Buddhist commandments."

However, I do believe that in order to lead a life of holiness—

translate that to "an enlightened life"—we have to follow certain universal natural laws of behavior. Since some of these laws are covered in the Five Wonderful Precepts, perhaps I could accept them as spiritual rules of conduct basic to most religious ways of life.

Struggling again over my decision, I wanted to go back to sleep. As I enlisted my meditative breathing to still me into relaxation, I wondered and vacillated. Even if there are universal spiritual laws, maybe I would be recklessly visiting one tradition while being faithful to another. The Bible warns against mixing wool and linen, and forbids plowing with an ox and a donkey together (Deuteronomy 22:9-11), prohibitions that apply not only to these specifics but "to any coupling of species, for any kind of work," according to the great rabbinical commentator known as Rashi. How much more dangerous is it to blend Buddhism and Judaism? Now, in the middle of the night, as I was again rehashing the struggles of the previous day, I was getting sleepy.

My pencil flashlight seemed like a needle probing some large stack of loose associations, a dare against a foreign body of beings. All lights blurred into the same strange landscape of my dream with Thây. I drifted into an image of myself in a dark long coat, similar to the garb that Thây wore when he glided through my dreamscape. I felt an inner defiant urge that exploded into five replicas of myself as anxiety tore me apart at the seams. Strangely I was drawn to the antique protruding rollers of a four-legged washing machine. It was like the one my landlady let me use during graduate school. The rollers pulled me through them continually and magically until there were five of me. Suddenly that same eye from the previous dream saw five of my selves hung out to dry on a circular clothesline that spun round like a merry-go-round. Round and round these selves spun, while I heard a voice declaring, "Hungry ghosts, hungry ghosts!" Hungry ghosts in Buddhism describe unsatisfied souls who wander through *samsara*, this world of delusion with its continual process of birth, death, and rebirth, trying to fulfill their missions.

"What is it now?" asked my poor, patient, and sympathetic

roommate, surprised in her sleep. Even though she was startled by my fear into speaking, I tried not to answer because we were supposed to maintain the rule of silence. Silence hung over us in the room as the moonlight faded and the sky lightened.

Tossing and turning as the sun slowly brightened the skylight above our bed, I recounted yesterday's Dharma discussion to raise questions and dispel doubts. A veteran of the encounter wars of the sixties and seventies, and the milder varieties of corporate workshops in the eighties, I did not know what to expect in this setting. Sister Eleni and Sister Annabel, a lady with an English accent and regal bearing, were the two leaders. Almost twelve of us, silent as apostles in training, sat in a circle. We were to press hands together and nod our heads before and after our comments, and the group would respond as respectfully. This was called a bow but seemed to me only a quaint but appealing Asian curtsy. Eleni bowed and explained and invited questions; she bowed again to punctuate the end of her introduction.

I waited and then asked about mosquitoes. In the hit-or-get-bit world of summer gardening, what does one do to uphold the precept against killing? Everyone in the group claimed they had the same problem. Or were they just putting me on? A handsome long-haired thirty-something man with Chinese features and the bearing of an Indian warrior on a horse, suggested an environmentally sensitive lotion to repel these sentient beings.

After a silence, a burly British tenor bowed and addressed the group from some old bowl of pain in his belly. His voice and jaw became tighter and tighter, his shoulders raised higher and higher with tension, as he told the story of holding a woman dying in childbirth; she was a tribal outcast because of her illegitimate pregnancy. (Inadvertently I flashed to my mother's weeping tale of the loss of her first newborn, a son, to some midwife's incompetence in Grodno.) Now, however, this poor man looked like someone resisting birth pangs himself. Red-faced, he resisted breathing and gasped for air. On his left, a slightly graying handsome Belgian psychiatrist held his hand and arm; on his right, a white-haired seventy-something muscular New Zealander, newly wed, held his other arm. Amid a silent cast of characters, I sat directly across from him as his eyes became more and more bloodshot. If only he could let himself cry.

A therapeutic response from my former paraprofessional days as a Gestalt counselor sparked me to move. As I put my hands with a slight pressure on the trapezius muscle holding his neck to his shoulders, I breathed with a studied evenness and hoped that he would hear and follow me. *Oh please Mr. Big Man with the largest muscles and body I had ever encountered o you like a sailor a foreign legionnaire o with so much resistance listen to the relaxation in the breath and clean the silence with the hope of your breath.*

The whole group breathed with me—or was I breathing the whole group? The quiet spanned a century of cultures and geography and age with our common empathy for this big man.

Like a coyote addressing the moon, a call broke and sang from someone's chest. With a rhythm of the American West, of the wild, wild West, with a call and a break and the dance on a tongue, this Chinese Indian warrior called for a god to come down to help. On and on, and again the *howwwls* broke and sang to help this poor big man

Thanks be to G-d, he finally relaxed and found his breath and the natural color of his face. Begging our forgiveness, he remained embarrassed even through my moist-eyed farewell to him and everyone's good wishes afterward. He immediately left for home to be with his partner. There was a dignity in the reception of his pain without any demand for explanation that I hadn't found in all those previous new age panaceas of emotional materialism.

During this restless night of flashbacks and dreams, I empathized with his struggle, and as I tried to rise from my pallet, I did not welcome the morning silence. I wanted to settle myself. Enough of challah mice, separate selves, Indian calls, and personal struggles! I wanted to talk to someone. I worried about how the work-sergeant nun would react to today's Shabbat restriction from work. On the very first day I had rejected the offer of rest for my jet lag. I was given a greenhouse to clean and did so vigorously; I had helped in the kitchen and cleaned our bathrooms without prodding.

Now I hastened in silence to the assignment board, which had me cleaning the bathrooms in my dormitory. I ate breakfast quickly and hurried back to sit on the stairs opposite the bathrooms with my Chumash (a compilation of the first five books of the Bible and readings from the Prophets, organized in the order of the weekly Torah portions) and Sabbath prayerbook on my lap while I began to pray the Sabbath prayers and hoped a solution would follow. At that moment my roommate Peggy came out with yellow rubber gloves carrying a pail! Wordless, she waved me upstairs without any reference to our difficult night. Working meditation also maintained a Sangha silence.

Blessing her kindness, I obeyed and went to our room, where I recited the Sabbath morning prayers and the weekly reading from the Torah. Personal memories and my personal theology often mix with rabbinical commentaries during this weekly ritual. The portion for this morning (Exodus 27:20–30:10) was called *Tetzaveh,* from the first Hebrew word of the portion, "You shall command." The Holy One addresses Moses and explains the 613 Jewish commandments. Twelve years ago, at my younger daughter's bat mitzvah, my husband began reading these very words from the Torah parchment scroll at Temple Beth El in Sudbury. The rules for keeping the eternal light burning in the Temple begin this passage with overreaching meaning to one's own eternal light of faith. This is the light that the Syrians spoiled in the Temple, for which the Maccabeans only found enough oil for one day and yet the light burned for eight, the light that the victory of Chanukkah celebrates, the light that we commemorate in our Friday night lighting of candles. I thought of that old saying "Keep the home fires burning." Now I wondered where I could find my own light, my own spark of holiness in this far-from-home village.

Tetzaveh describes the priests' vestments (no longer used by Jews since the destruction of the Holy Temple but imitated in the robes of Catholic priests), the architecture and furnishings of the portable temple, the Tabernacle, in the wilderness. I have often thought that the Torah portion of the week into which one is born is an astrological message relevant to our personality and our life lesson. For example, this portion about clothing, furnishings, and their use was given to my younger daughter, who loves all the fancy furnishings of life. My portion includes the Song of the Sea in Exodus 15, sung after the escape from slavery through the parting of the waves of the Red Sea. My life seems to be a constant struggle against the false ideas that enslave me. I am continually refining my personal theology, even here in Plum Village.

Some Jews use the weekly Torah portion like a personal *I Ching* to solve their current problems. This Sabbath's portion described the Israelites' form of divination, called the Urim and Thumim ("lightings and perfections"), housed in a fold in the high priest's golden breastplate, in which was embedded a jewel for each of the twelve tribes of Israel. The commentators Rashi and Rambam thought that the Urim and Thumim were a mystical name or names of G-d, but their exact appearance is not known. The Vilna Gaon describes how the high priest would face the altar and ask the supplicant's question, and then the jewels on the front of the breastplate would light up with a coded answer. In Samuel 28:6, according to Everett Fox, a recent translator of the Five Books of Moses, the Urim and Thumim "are equated with dreams and prophecies as a means of answering human queries." I wished I could ask that oracle now what seeds my adventures were watering for the future.

I put my prayerbook and Bible back in my luggage and returned to my struggle over the vowing and bowing. The precepts ceremony also included a promise to uphold the three refuges, "Buddha, Dharma, and Sangha." This would be going too far for me! I sought help and finally found Sister Annabel, who agreed to discuss my reservations. I told her that one's word is considered to be like a written contract. Once a vow is made, one cannot be released from it without great difficulty. When making a promise or even booking an appointment, observant Jews add the Hebrew phrase *b'li neder*, which means "without a vow," because we never can predict what will occur to interfere with the best of intentions. In a word, we don't make promises lightly.

"Catholics raise the same issues," replied Sister Annabel as if she knew the experience. She offered a solution to my struggle. "I can substitute the word *aspire* for *vow* in the precepts ceremony, if that is acceptable to you." That would work, so I complied.

"There is, however, the problem of bowing down to an image or person," I said. "Jews can't do that. The second commandment says that we cannot bow down to any graven image or have any other gods." Since bowing would dishonor my ancestors to whom I must pay respect, she suggested that just touching the ground instead of prostrating would be acceptable for the ceremony. Apparently, I was not the first to object to this, and Thây strove for universal inclusiveness.

I had to voice all reservations. Even though Buddhists claim that Buddhism is not a religion, I could not dedicate myself to the Buddha, the Dharma, and the Sangha, the three refuges that were foreign to me; I needed at least to substitute Hebrew equivalents. Sister Annabel asked what words I would choose.

Since *Buddha* was the example of the unending mystical state of awakening and enlightenment, I suggested one of the mystical Hebrew names for G-d: Ayn Sof, the One without End. This quality has no beginning, no middle, and no ending, but is always enlightened; it is the quality that was there before creation and is forever. Sister Annabel agreed.

Dharma means the teaching of the Buddha. Jews follow the Torah the way Buddhists follow the Dharma, so I would substitute *Torah* and add *Halakhah*, literally the path that one walks: the complete body of laws that Jews are bound to follow, including biblical commandments, rules instituted by the rabbis, and binding customs. She had no objections here.

For *Sangha*, the Buddhist community, I could use *Kehillah*, or congregation, and *Chavurah*, the community and fellowship of friends. No problem here.

We ended our meeting amicably, and Sister Annabel bowed and

left. I checked the schedule for the time of the ceremony and waited impatiently for Ben.

Finally, he arrived by van from the men's hamlet. I reviewed Annabel's suggestions and he smiled. He, of course, had no compunctions about the terminology or taking vows here. A bell told us to assemble in the zendo. We entered the sanctuary together with several candidates to meditate before the Precept Recitation Ceremony. The silence calmed me as I listened to my heart slow down. I knew from experience that if I could just concentrate on my breath, then my emotions, sensations, and thoughts would enter my consciousness, rise, and fall. Observing this mind-stream was observing transformation.

Sister Annabel began with the incense offering: "In gratitude, we offer this incense to all Buddhas and Bodhisattvas throughout space and time. May it be fragrant as Earth herself, reflecting our careful efforts, our wholehearted awareness, and the fruit of understanding, slowly ripening." I recalled the description in Exodus about incense as an "odor pleasing to the Lord."

Next came six bows full face flat on the ground, each punctuated with the bell, to various Bodhisattvas, to the children, and to the "stream of ancestral teachers, to whom we bow in gratitude." My scalp went wet and hot—a reaction I'd had since childhood during emotional conflicts—as I touched the ground and faced the front of the room. *My* stream of realized teachers included Rabbi Akiva, whose skin was torn off because he would not bow to the oppressive law of the Romans, who forbade the teaching of Torah; the Baal Shem Tov, founder of the mystical Hasidic movement; and the original Lubavitcher Rebbe, Rabbi Shneur Zalman, who wrote exactingly about the various levels of mystical consciousness in his book, the *Tanya*. I knew very well that these sages would never want me to bow.

So I didn't.

But why was I allowing myself to come so close to apostasy? It was because I wanted to be as close to Ben in his experience as possible, because I wanted to understand my son.

With an orchestration that sounded like High Mass, Sister

Annabel began the chanting a Buddhist sutra first in its original language, "*Namo tassa* . . . ," and then in English:

> The Dharma is deep and lovely.
> We now have a chance to see it,
> study it, and practice it.
> We vow to realize its true meaning.

Annabel was vowing it; I substituted the word "aspire" as she had suggested.

And then came the chant of *Heart of the Prajñaparamita* (also known as the Heart Sutra, one of the forty sutras that make up the *Prajñaparamita Sutra*), which declares:

> Form is no other than emptiness;
> Emptiness is no other than form.

This is the central Buddhist notion of emptiness, which Thây teaches as Interbeing. All feelings, perceptions, mental formations, and consciousness come from emptiness. This certainly sounded like the Ayn Sof, the G-d of no end. In *Zen Bones*, Thây describes emptiness, *shunyata*, derived from the notion of no-self. To him, being "empty of a separate self means full of everything!' *Ayn*, the Hebrew for Nothingness, is described by the Kabbalists as being the highest form of transcendence. Rabbi Aryeh Kaplan, in *Meditation and Kabbalah*, says: "Actually, this alludes to the ultimate level reached by non-directed meditation, where all perception and imagery cease to exist." Both seem to be referring to an ultimate state, the Divine Source, in which I could take refuge.

The chanting, the sound of "*Gate gate paragate* . . . ," fell over me like a hypnotic spell; the repetitive resonance of the bells, accompanied by Sister Annabel's singing, was enchanting. Again, it was like High Mass at Nôtre Dame Cathedral in Paris as our lady of a cappella, Annabel, intoned the three refuges: Buddha, the one who shows the way; Dharma, the way of understanding and love; and Sangha, the community that lives in harmony and awareness.

As for me, I took refuge in Ayn Sof, the mystical name of G-d without End; Torah and Halakhah, the Law and its ways; and Kehillah and Chavurah, the community and the fellowship of friends.

She read each of the five precepts and then asked us, after each one, to promise to study each one. When she said "vow," I whispered "aspire" to myself each time, and each time the bell rang in agreement. For the first time during my stay, I raised my eyes to face the Buddha at the front of the room. On the chest of this golden larger-than-life image was a frieze that I had never noticed until now. Its golden chest had the embossed symbol of what appeared to be a swastika! I considering bolting from the room, but this would embarrass Ben and disturb the dignity of the others. I had not discussed this with Annabel because I had not noticed it before. My scalp was wet and blazing. A flashlight on my consciousness, I searched for an escape. Even though I believed in the principles behind the precepts, this symbol had shaken me.

Thây says that every part of life should be a meditation, so I breathed lightly, and I tried to meditate on this symbol. "Deep looking" was what he called that process. Annabel's voice passed through me like breath as I focused on the frieze. A new thought entered my mind: Wasn't this some sort of ancient Buddhist symbol that predated the Nazis? I surely hoped that was it. The Nazis came much later and, I had heard, in their perversity they reversed the direction of the arms of this auspicious symbol. No wonder it ran them into the ground and defeat. My magical thinking brought me relief! I was not going to mess with this stuff, so I kept still until I received my certificate. After more bells and chanting, we left the sanctuary walking slowly and respectfully in a meditative posture.

In the back of the sanctuary, I tried to read the Vietnamese name that I had been given. It was written in the Latin alphabet with French accents, a conversion from the Vietnamese characters, made during the French occupation of Vietnam. The name,

Nguyên Thông, was translated on my certificate as "Communion of the Source." I guessed that Sister Annabel (or Bhikshuni True Virtue) had translated this. I was required to read the five precepts every three months or lose my title. They certainly believed in the honor principle.

After the concluding chants, we backed out of the zendo.

Later I learned that the frieze on the Buddha's chest was a symbol of Buddha's wheel of teaching (*dharma-chakra*). In Sanskrit *svastika* means "conducive to well-being," and this ancient sign was popular in both Hinduism and Buddhism. It appeared as a positive symbol in ancient Scandinavian, early Christian, and Native American traditions as well. Contrary to popular belief, the swastika appears in Asian iconography with its arms in both clockwise and counterclockwise directions; the Nazis did not "reverse" the symbol. They adopted the clockwise swastika, regarded as a solar image representing the daily movement of the sun through the heavens, as the symbol for their anti-Semitic political party.

Although at Plum Village Ben reassured me about the original Buddhist meaning of the swastika, still I asked myself what had I done. What garb had I donned? Was the five-selved dream about my compatibility with the five precepts? Following the precepts was not against my beliefs, but the ceremony left me stunned. Our common experience, our agreement over the universal meaning of the precepts, and our continuing discussion of the precepts brought me closer to Ben. While this was my journey's goal, the struggle had surely washed something out of me.

However, I didn't realize that the ceremony might bring me closer to a meeting with Thây.

7

Tea with a Zen Master

AFTER MY ACCEPTANCE OF THE FIVE WONDERFUL PRE-
cepts, no dreams visited me and the nights became one unified,
uninterrupted pattern of sleep. This morning's light, however,
brightened with a persistent memory of past dreamtimes. Against
the herringbone wood slat wall of my room, I saw again the most
vivid dream of my life. Twenty years ago, when I was near death
from a life-threatening illness, my dream was more real than life.
Floating out of my body, I rose up, up, and up inside the clouds
above. With no door visible, I nevertheless knocked, repeatedly
demanding entry. The sky whitened with my greeting as a Large
Voice stated, "You have got a lot of work to do." It sent me down,
down back into my body with the life-long question: What is
my Work (with a capital W)? Is my present action leading to
my Work?

At the time of the dream my personal life was in disarray and
distracted my focus for the Work, whatever that was. Afterward,
my Jewish spiritual tradition guided my recovery and helped me
to mend my personal and familial relationships as much as I

could. However, my past journeys to the dark side had wounded my children. Now they mainly confided in their father, while I was constantly learning and earning their closeness. This journey to understand my Buddhist son's spiritual path was part of that learning and, unexpectedly, was teaching me more about myself than I had anticipated.

Ben was, like Thây's description of the new nun and monk, "an ambassador from the Buddha-land whose one letter home can bring awakened understanding." By bringing me with him on this journey, Ben was reaching out to me as he had reached out to the whole family from his retreat.

During Thây's same teaching after the ordination, he said, "We are not just there for ourselves, but for everybody else: the people we love, the people we hate, the people we don't love, and the people that we are not yet able to love."

The people that we are not yet able to love.

This unique way of looking at those who have betrayed us, angered us, or even merely annoyed us, demonstrates Thây's faith in everyone's ability to love everyone else. I pictured the people I had once hated for their bad influence, seducing members of my family away from the family. I thought of the anger I once felt for my husband, blaming his explorations of New Age paths for my afflictions, resenting my caretaker role while he went to California to be with his guru of the moment, whether the mystic-philosopher-scientist Franklin Merrell-Wolff or Krishnamurti. How ironic now for me to be seeking an audience with a guru. While planning for our trip, Ben had mentioned that Thây might agree to see us if it would foster harmony in the mother-son relationship. I wrote him a long letter about it and daydreamed of a theological cross-cultural exchange, from Ben's description of Thây's ecumenical nature.

Thây taught that one should practice reconciliation in the face of anger, how the other person doesn't have to be present, and, most important of all, how to use meditation to disarm ourselves, to look deeply into our own heart and transform it. Then others will see by the light in our eyes that we have changed and that they are no longer the object of our anger. Change yourself and you change the world. Once more Thây described the methodology called mindfulness, deep looking, deep listening, and the transformational power of meditation. From this, compassion arises.

I had never looked deeply at how my husband and I had disarmed until I heard Thây's teaching. The change in our marriage must have occurred in a similar way: separately we prayed daily, and separately we tried to build our lives long after couples' therapy had played itself out. We had disarmed ourselves separately; I finally realized from his eyes that he really saw me and liked the person he saw. Subsequently, by sorting out our separate realities, we learned that, as Thây had taught, we were both "victims of wrong perceptions." The anger *had* left me. Now I couldn't imagine hating him anymore; my husband had gradually become, again, the guy I met over forty years ago when we both knew we would marry and have a life together. We are finally having that life. Hail to the empty nest!

I also began to look deeply at my mother's suffering and realized that, as Thây said, she didn't have the luck to have the seeds of happiness watered; the murder of her family in the Holocaust, and the deaths of her children, my siblings, and then my father, haunted her continually. They continue even after her death to affect me.

Yet ironically now I was seeking an audience with a teacher, not to find the Ultimate Answer—the motivation for my husband's explorations of New Age philosophies—but to understand what my son had found in these philosophies. Thây, in his tapes that Ben had sent me, not only described my own experience and aspirations, but he also made me feel that peace is possible "with every step." The key was daily practice of meditation and "right-mindedness." By meditating on the principles of compassion, one could begin the path of right-mindedness. From right-mindedness comes concentration, or focus. With focus, perhaps I could begin my Work as instructed in my dream. Concentration, according to Thây, leads to awakened understanding, and from this comes the insight of a free person. Some people may learn in an instant, says Thây, and others may never get it in their entire lives. I wanted to meet with Thây to understand more of this, and how to reconcile myself with Ben's path.

After pondering these thoughts during breakfast, I found myself in a conversation with Sister True Emptiness, Thây's longtime colleague. She was speaking to me about my requested meeting with Thây. She asked me about my background, so I told her how I use the Jewish Sabbath to pray, study, and meditate alone. Lately I had become more Orthodox in my observance, abstaining from driving and the wasteful use of electricity. I described how sometimes, late Saturday afternoon, my consciousness shifts. A new direction enters, a problem gets solved, a picture comes to me, and something inside opens. As I described this process, something seemed to change in her eyes; perhaps a decision was silently made. Nevertheless, my incessant curiosity drove me to ask many questions about Jewish-Buddhist similarities.

"Fax your questions to me at Thây's hut," she said as she turned and left. And so I faxed questions about the dialogue between the two religions, about how the source seems similar, and about my qualms about the Buddhist custom of prostration. I wrote:

One of the Ten Commandments in the Old Testament says, "Thou shalt not bow down to any other gods or idols." This represents the belief in the ONEness of the Creating Energy. The commandment also specifies that we are not to make any images of the ONE. How can this be reconciled with the Buddhist practice of using images?

In the *Tanya,* the book that I will give you by the Lubavitcher Rebbe, it says that we are encumbered by "klippot" (Hebrew for outer layers). It says that our true nature (the Holy Spark, created at the time of creation) is hidden under these layers. Is there anything like this in Buddhism?

The following day, in nervous anticipation, I rode the van to the Lower Hamlet for Thây's next Dharma talk. I entered a building full of cameras, microphones, sound boxes, and thin angel-hair wires strung to each participant's chair for the simultaneous English translation of Thây's Vietnamese. The Vietnamese nuns, monks, and residents sat together, unencumbered by the electronic paraphernalia that the rest of us needed for for translation.

Sister True Emptiness entered and came right up to me. She told me that she was pleased about my accepting the Five Wonderful Precepts. I took the opportunity to ask about the pronunciation of the name given to me during the ceremony. She engaged the entire group of Asian monks to demonstrate the pronunciation and help translate the name, Nguyên Thông. *New-hen Tohm*, with French nasality and a melodious lilt, is how I heard it. The newly formed committee buzzed over the accuracy of its English translation as "Communion of the Source." After an animated group discussion in Vietnamese, and after much nodding and naying of heads, they finally told Sister True Emptiness their official verdict:

"Going-through-Obstacles-to-the-Source!"

Was my life that obvious?

Thây entered smiling, and we all rose. We watched him take off his coat, settle into his chair, and adjust his microphone. In days of old, disciples would learn by watching how their master tied his shoelaces. Today they watch as he adjusts the wire from his microphone to the power box.

Thây's teaching, punctuated periodically by the usual bell reminder, arrived in my headphones through the whispered English accent of Sister Annabel. He began with a description of himself as an impatient youth running up the stairs four at a time because "we thought happiness was in the future. But," he emphasized, "that is throwing away the life of the present moment." He talked about the value of walking meditation as an anchor in discovering the present moment. Elsewhere, he had recommended using walking meditation when feelings were too strong to hold in sitting meditation. The miracle is not, according to Thây, to walk on water, but "to walk on the earth."

He described how mindfulness in every body of experience naturally waters the seeds of the next body and allows them to bloom; these seeds are naturally present in all of us because "the Buddha in our hearts knows this." Thây described how "deep listening" enables concentration and fosters understanding; how, from this, insight springs; and how this gets us in touch with the seeds of our store-consciousness, the repository of all ideas, feelings, and paradigms. He seemed to be describing my first Plum Village dream with the large seed-pod sparked to life by Thây.

I began to think about the fictional Hasidic Rabbi Saunders in Chaim Potok's novel *The Chosen*, who was continually silent toward his brilliant but arrogant son, Danny. I wondered if his silence was intended to water the seeds in Danny's store-consciousness. Perhaps he was acting like a Dharma master, teaching Danny to hear through deep listening "the pain of the world," to foster compassion and even enlightenment, insight, and wisdom. After all, Danny was being groomed to take his father's place as head of the Hasidic dynasty. Ultimately the rabbi would discover that Danny had a forbidden friend, Reuven Malter, the son of a humanist Zionist, a professor who was feeding Danny a steady diet of books from science to Shakespeare. Danny, however, wanted to use his deep listening to be a psychologist.

My attention returned to Thây, who was now describing the Buddhist practice of prostration. Once, when a group of Vietnamese delegates, finally able to leave the Communist-dominated North for a visit with him, were not at ease prostrating to the Buddha because of their atheistic environment, he told them: "This practice is not superstition but based on our faith." Was he answering the question about the necessity of prostration that I had faxed to him the previous day?

Prostration, he continued, establishes a relationship of love and respect for parents, ancestors, and teachers. By prostrating we "drop the idea of self and become one with a whole line of ancestors," just as "when we pray to G-d, we give up the idea of a separate being."

Perhaps, when I balked at prostrating and was asked to stoop and just touch the earth, that gesture indicated this union of the self with all who went before. Even so, it was incompatible with modern Judaism. But how, then, I wondered, could the two religions dialogue?

"You cannot have a dialogue of two religions unless you are liberated in your own religion." Thây seemed to read my mind.

This attitude would lessen the suffering between religions. According to a *New York Times* article, he had once demonstrated this teaching during a New York retreat by encouraging his Jewish followers to observe Yom Kippur. "Suffering," Thây continued, "will grow weaker and be transformed." That is, if we don't nourish it: "The more we complain of suffering, the more the seed of suffering is watered." This philosophy would certainly drive many therapists out of business.

"The teacher," said Thây, putting one hand on his heart, "takes the seal from his heart"—he put his other hand on the heart of a nearby monk—"and impresses it on the heart of his disciple. The disciple then has to transmit the heart to his disciples. He can do this because his heart is not covered by plastic. The transmission has to be from heart to heart. . . . This is called the Seal of the Heart."

Rabbi Nachman of Breslov, a great Ukrainian Hasidic mystical master of the early nineteenth century, talked of the imprint of the master on his student in a similar way. Both gurus had similar teaching modes.

I was so engrossed in my own thoughts and comparisons that I didn't notice when the Dharma talk was over. Suddenly, everyone was being ushered toward an elaborate buffet for a formal vegetarian dinner. The Vietnamese cooks had produced an impressive array with their various gluten-based meat substitutes and homemade noodles. Some dishes resembled roast stuffed veal, others looked like barbecued beef. There were numerous vegetable presentations and warm miso soup; the teas were fruity and aromatic. I was delighted not to have any conflict with my kosher food habits. With my plate heaped high with food, I joined a silent line to the sanctuary where about a hundred nuns, monks, residents, and visitors sat cross-legged on meditation pillows and mats for the formal meal. The Japanese Zen master with the brown breastplate had returned to his school in Germany, the home of many Vietnamese after the war. I felt disappointed not to be able to admire his bearing and presence again.

We ate in silent meditation until the entertainment began. Fond of cross-cultural entertainment, Thây introduced Sister True Emptiness and her melodic soprano English rendition of a German song. A monk sang the song in its original German. Other news and conversation followed in the formal measured beat of an Oriental tea ceremony. The dinner ended as another announcement was made:

"Thây will have an interview with Ben and his mother at four-thirty."

I became speechless and nervous as Ben walked to my side from across the room.

Now, I am not the let-us-now-praise-famous-men type, with an autograph pad in hand. Rather I am the find-the-chink-in-the-armor and question-everything type. I once reprimanded Fritz Perls, the founder of Gestalt therapy, for his womanizing after I mistook him (jokingly) for a janitor at the Esalen Institute. At nineteen, I chided the playwright Arthur Miller when, addressing the American Psychological Association, he overidealized artists (they would never drop a bomb on Hiroshima!); and, in my thirties on Martha's Vineyard, I scolded Ram Dass (the former Richard Alpert), at the beginning of his career as a wise man, for not studying the Talmud.

Until now, only a brief meeting with the late Lubavitcher Rebbe, Rabbi Menachem Shneerson, in Crown Heights had filled me with wordless awe. For Thây I was indeed nervous all afternoon. At 4:30, Sister True Emptiness led us through the dining hall to a small stone building with a small room off the front hallway, where she answered my faxed questions. She confirmed that the parallels I had suggested did exist in Judaism and Buddhism. For example, the divine sparks described in kabbalistic writings could be a parallel to certain seeds of enlightenment in the Buddhist store-consciousness.

I was thrilled to be sitting next to a heroine of the Vietnam War, a peace activist herself, and a founder with Thây of the Vietnamese School of Youth for Social Service and the Order of Interbeing, "created by Thây to help bring Buddhism directly into the arena of social concerns during a time when the war was escalating and the teachings of the Buddha were most sorely needed." Her closest sister in the Dharma, Nhat Chi Mai, whom she had persuaded to join the work for peace at Van Hanh University, protested the Vietnam War with the personal sacrifice of self-immolation on May 14, 1967. Before her act of self-sacrifice, she read a poem of Thây's. I remembered seeing a newspaper photo of a nun's self-immolation and had carried the memory of that flaming woman martyr with me for a long time. It may well have been Sister Mai.

When it was time to go in the next room, we saw Thây folding a string hammock that he had unhooked from the ceiling. Laden with my heavy backpack and a bag full of expectations, I entered and Thây smiled at me. For the first time I looked closely at him. He resembled an elf with a close-shaven head; he appeared to me both Asian in his stature and Western in his features. Peggy, my roommate, had said he looked like Yoda, the *Star Wars* movie guru, with the look of a newborn baby, wizened as well as childlike and innocent. He was so very petite, reminding me how I had read in *The Ugly American* that the Vietnamese thought Americans seemed like clumsy klutzes.

Thây motioned toward the pile of pillows; as I lowered myself quickly without grace, my knee pierced me with pain. He helped me rearrange myself and urged me with compassion to take care of myself. Slowly I undid my gear while Ben, familiar with the etiquette, expressed gratitude for Thây's teachings.

"My mother and I have known much suffering," Ben began, "but I have studied your teachings through your books and tapes, and I have been able to appreciate her. I want to thank you for your teachings." Ben bowed. Thây bowed also, and then he turned to look at me. As I was groping for the proper presentation, Ben knew what would please. "My mother has taken the Five Precepts," he added. Thây nodded with a smile.

"And I have explained to her," added Sister True Emptiness, "as you said about the bowing down, the touching the earth, our source, and she understands and is willing to do it."

"Only if there is no Buddha!" I exclaimed, surprised by her conclusion. I hoped that I had not ruined our first meeting with this outburst.

"You see," Ben rushed to explain, "one of the early Jewish ancestors was Abraham, who was the son of an idol-maker. One day he destroyed the idols in his father's shop—all but one. When his father came home and asked who did this, Abraham pointed to the last intact idol and said that this idol did it. 'How could that be?' asked Abraham's father; 'he is only an image.' 'Then,' answered Abraham, 'why do you worship him?' Since then, because of Abraham, Jews don't bow down to images." It surprised and pleased me that he knew the rabbinical commentary on this point.

"Yes," Thây said, "people have false expectations, that people should behave in a certain way, that children should be a certain way. . . ." His voice trailed off as Ben put his finger on my calf, very gently, very significantly. *This* was not like the usual rabbinical commentary on the subject. Thây's conclusions awoke me like a koan-midrash! He had addressed the larger, unspoken issue of making our children follow our own image. I did not expect this turn of meaning on myself.

Quiet returned to the room. Caught again by Thây's gaze, I was stilled by his dark brown eyes, so perfect for his features. His presence was as delicate as a feather floating on a breath in midair, but he was grounded in his lotus posture, holding his hands together in a gesture that resembled a flower.

As the time ripened for me to speak, I became even more nervous. I chattered endlessly, describing my night dreams in Plum Village. He listened deeply but made no sound. Mesmerized by his gaze, I was the last to notice that tea had been poured for us, and I was the last to notice that Thây had already lifted his cup to the

palm of the other hand, which served as a saucer. The others—
Ben, Sister True Emptiness, and Thây's attendant—had followed
their teacher's example, and each had raised his or her own cup of
tea as they watched me. I looked at my full cup on the table and
wondered if I had committed another rudeness in the presence of
this venerable teacher. Now in this present moment with this Zen
master, I was to learn to do one thing at a time, something quite
foreign to me. Here he was, breathing, not in a waiting way, holding his small cup of tea in the palm of his hand, ready to sip his tea;
it would be rude of him to do so while I was talking.

So I finally stopped talking.

He slowly sipped his tea; the others followed with one simultaneous movement around that small table on the floor. I became
caught in this common motion.

For one extraordinary moment it seemed that I had come only
for tea, to be in this ceremony with this teacher and his entourage,
and just enjoy the company and the warmth of the tea and our
hands cupping the teacups on this damp, rainy day, to breathe
easily and say nothing, to do no more than this. All else was commentary, as Rabbi Hillel said.

"Very interesting." Thây said when the time was ripe. I had almost forgotten what we were talking about. Oh yes, my dream.

Simultaneously we all sipped our tea again in the dance of the
tea ceremony. Maybe the dream was about this very moment.

Again I was caught in his eyes. I breathed.

"Do you interpret dreams?" I finally asked. He looked at Sister
True Emptiness briefly.

"The meaning," he finally said as I held my breath, "will ripen
—in time."

Remembering that I had brought a gift, I clumsily emptied the
contents of my backpack. A picture of my husband holding our
grandsons, Max and Levi, dropped out; I must have thrown it
into my backpack for courage. Embarrassed, I watched Thây
bow to them as if he were being introduced. While Ben caught
the tape recorder that fell from my pack and set it up, I presented
the gift. Carefully and respectfully, Thây unwrapped the pack-

age, damaged in transit, to uncover the book. It was the *Tanya,* a work of Jewish mysticism by the original Lubavitcher Rebbe, Shneur Zalman of Liadi, first published in 1796. It described how every soul desires to be reunited with G-d, the Source of all life, but is bound in this life by the *klippot,* the "shells" of flesh and blood that conceals the divine life force or spark inside each of us since Creation. These *klippot* function like the peel that conceals a fruit. I thought that Thây's brilliant poetic mind might be interested in the *Tanya*'s detailed explanations of these technicalities of Jewish mysticism. His interest did prod him to open it from time to time and glance at it during our discussion. To some, this anthology of the Alter Rebbe's discourses was an extended prose poem describing the images and metaphors of Jewish mysticism. To his followers, it was not only a spiritual agenda for the Jewish people but also the definitive Jewish spiritual manual on practical and religious ethics.

I held my notebook tightly in my lap; I didn't want to disturb the stillness with the rustling of paper, or the scratch of the pen. I reached out for this silence like a sleepwalker who instinctively knows the way. My next gift was in my notebook. During yesterday's walking meditation that Thây led through the just-beginning blossoms of the plum orchard, a poem sprang out. I read it to him now:

> The wind
> gentled to a breeze
> is you
> touching
> the sun
> in seeds

He accepted this also with a bow and an air of detachment. I guess the poem is not very good, I thought.

Just then Thây looked at the tape recorder on the table near the vase with one lone flower on a branch of moss. Thây touched the machine and said, "This is a flower." Then pointing to the flower in the vase, he said, "And this is a flower." Ben later told me the point of this was to show that both were listening. It is also a reminder of the story of the Buddha, who once, instead of giving a verbal teaching, only held a flower in silence.

"And," I added, "my name is a flower." He looked surprised and smiled spontaneously. But was *this* flower, Rosie, listening as she rustled on her pillow trying to ignore the heat in her knee? Later Ben wrote my husband that my continuous chatter surprised him.

"Now, what is your question?" he asked.

"I have so many."

"Just the most important question." I thought of Ben and me, but he had already spoken to our relationship when he spoke about expectations; he had also addressed my faxed questions in this morning's teachings. I waited for the words to ripen, but a flood of questions rose up.

"How can we bring the religions together? What can I do to help?" I got two questions in. Later I realized that I was generalizing my own personal concern into a global issue.

"Why do you want to do that?" Surprised, I caught my breath and fell into his gaze; his brown eyes were so dark that I couldn't see their irises. I had no answer, no shorthand, no language to fathom the meaning of his question; it seemed too deep for my words. He sipped his tea. We all mirrored his movements and sipped our tea.

"Did you enjoy your lunch?" he asked again.

"I loved it!"

"Perhaps it would be better for all the religions to enjoy a meal together."

"If only we could agree on the menu," I said, thinking about the kosher considerations.

I persisted and showed him my traveling prayerbook. I asked, "What about including mindfulness exercises in Jewish prayerbooks?" Since I had contributed to prayerbooks in the past, I imagined somehow incorporating moments of mindfulness into

Jewish prayer, perhaps to allow us to savor the words more. He listened with his eyes.

"We have very little ritual in Plum Village," he said, touching the dog-eared cover.

"These aren't rituals. They're prayers."

Disappointment pulled me into the ground. I had overreached, and now it was time to go. Thây, however, consented to sign some of his books. When I handed him his first hand-bound volume of poems, the now out-of-print *Zen Poems*, he smiled fondly at it. That smile warmed my departure, even as I silently questioned the wisdom of this meeting. I also wondered what the most important question was, and whether I had asked it or just wasted my opportunity.

Thây agreed to pose for a photograph with me, but later Ben realized that there was neither film in the camera nor tape in the recorder.

Had I traveled over water, over land, by air, by train, and on foot, just to remember the warmth of the teacup in my hands, just to sip tea together in synchronicity, just to dissolve all thoughts and become lost in the dark pools of Thây's eyes—in a moment of what Thây calls Interbeing?

I still remember the light touch of his hand on my back, as we all faced the winking shutter of the ebony eye of my camera.

8

Laughing Meditation

As Sunday's light waned, my backpack became lighter and more manageable. After the meeting with Thây, Sister True Emptiness drove us to the formal tea ceremony already in progress for the Sangha, and then returned to him. We enjoyed tea poured meticulously and small sweets served graciously. The circle rustled with the shy but reserved revelry among the resident nuns and monks. By the custom of the village, visitors were invited to perform and add to its international flavor. Ben understood this, so he chanted in Tibetan in a deep, relaxed, and resonant voice that I had never heard before. A professional European singer sang an Austrian *Lied*; someone else sang a Christian hymn. They sounded so good that I felt inadequate to sing the song that I had rehearsed in Hebrew and English. Written by Rabbi Nachman, it contains these words:

> Life is but a very narrow bridge,
> but the main thing to recall
> is not to be afraid, not to be afraid at all.

Flustered, I read again the poem that I had written for Thây.

> The wind
> gentled to a breeze
> is you
> touching
> the sun
> in seeds

"What?" said the Vietnamese translator, who thought I had said either "seize" or "deeds." Everyone laughed. Giggling, I repeated it.

"Seas?" he asked, again laughing with every word. Because of the compact grammatical structure, he couldn't translate it. Another Vietnamese tried and failed; then a French woman tried and gave up. I tried to help by breaking it down into extended simple grammatical units. I had to deconstruct my own complicated and compact imagery to a giggling crowd.

"Well," I began giggling, "the poem's beginning image compares Thây to a wind that can become quiet, and that is how the wind becomes a breeze. You see, that's more gentle than a strong wind. That's what his presence and his teachings do. They make things gentle. So this wind, you see, comes by the seeds, and that's spelled *s-e-e-d-s*, the things that go into the ground to sprout plants, that's the kind of seeds that the poem is speaking of. Or you can interpret this as the seeds in our store-consciousness. Well, now, Thây, who is like a wind that's become gentle, brings out the whole wheel of life that is in the seed, and, in doing that, finds the sun that is in all the seeds. This refers to the teaching that says the flower is in the compost pile and in the compost pile is the cloud and the rain, and this becomes the seed and the compost that in turn is planted and becomes the flower again."

None of us could suppress our laughter. Ben's face was red with mirth. The Sangha's formal tea ceremony dissolved into a lightness of being. Quite by accident I became the embarrassed sit-down comic of that ecumenical crowd.

Afterward, as I walked, smiling, toward my room in the stone barn, I thought of Thây's description of the state of *samadhi,* and how it creates space around us and makes us feel lighter. "Samadhi," he explained, "is concentration, the mother who gives us awakened understanding. If we cannot live this life in right mindfulness and in concentration, we will never give rise to awakened understanding." The entire Sangha had experienced that feeling of lightness through laughter. Smiling, a movement that Thây constantly advocates, certainly makes us feel lighter. I thought of other moments that have the same cause, like the light that goes off in one's face at the realization of an insight, the first blush of love, or the feeling of understanding triggered by an insight about a situation or about people or even one's self. This same internal light may even shine in our face when we pursue an ideal or feel filled with doing something good. I was reminded of these words of Thây's from his tape *Call Me by My True Names*: "When a person is enlightened, there is light around him, and we like to say in my country that his traveling bags are full of moonlight."

Moonlight, I thought to myself as I looked up at the evening moon mist above me, was certainly lighter than the baggage I came with.

I kept thinking about Thây's specific description of sitting meditation during his last Dharma talk. By being "truly present" during sitting meditation, one is free, one is liberated. In the past, I had always used these terms in a political sense, as in the struggle for human rights, or Pharaoh's freeing of the Hebrew slaves. Thây had begun his talk with the question "Is anybody home?" I received it as a Zen koan. He explained that when one is present in the moment, there is "no past to oppress us or imprison us, and no future to pull us away. . . we let go of all heaviness from the past and attachments to the future. . . . We are truly a free human being. . . . So the next time someone asks, 'Is anybody at home?' say yes, we are really here at home, in the present moment."

I couldn't get this new definition of home out of my mind. As a sometime traveler, I always looked forward to arriving at my

home, my house where my dwelling is. To feel at home in a foreign land meant to be free. Was I experiencing a paradigm shift?
A new state of consciousness? This was too much thinking, even
for me. I shook my head as if to shake out old ideas.

Thankfully, the daily meditations created a calm in the Sangha
and me: with no urgent conflicts to disturb me and the meeting
with Thây over, I experienced an unbroken serenity with no more
disturbing night dreams. Even the mice let me sleep in peace. My
roommate also seemed grateful for uninterrupted sleep. The
Sangha surrounded us with the encouraging and reinforcing practices inherent in the compassionate ideals of the Order of Interbeing. Visitors were required to take part in all activities of the village: the walking, sitting, and working meditations, the silences,
the bell observances, the Dharma talks, the discussions, and the
ceremonies. All work and walking, conversation and meals,
moved in a meditative mode along with deep listening, deep looking, compassion, and deep understanding of others that arises
from mindful meditation.

My incessant curiosity still moved me, from time to time, to
think about the meaning of my five-self dream. I no longer felt
anxiety or fear about it or anything here. As a former paraprofessional counselor, not yet able to rid myself of the Gestalt idea of
giving voice to each part of my dream for its analysis, I raised my
puzzlement during our next Dharma discussion.

A monk was the facilitator this time, and he smiled when I
started to speak. I said I wanted to learn the Buddhist interpretation of dreams. The Jewish mystical approach to dreams as part
prophecy concerned me: was I so fragmented that I couldn't settle
on an approach, either mystical or psychological, to clarify this
mysterious scene from my unconscious? Again I described the
dream that caused me to wake my roommate, how I dared the
"Buddhist powers-that-be" and suddenly, how I watched myself
being washed, multiplied into five identical selves, and hung out
to dry on a clothesline accompanied by the cry: "Hungry ghosts!
Hungry ghosts!" These are beings plagued by insatiable appetites
who reincarnate into the Realm of Desire; they are one of the six

classes of beings represented on the Buddhist wheel of life, in the cycle of existence called samsara. To my comfort, however, I did not resemble these beings with their narrow necks, tiny mouths, and bulging stomachs. I did, however, have a great hunger for knowledge, for some bit of wisdom that would satisfy my surprise at the scene that arose in my dream.

After my narration, I paused and waited nervously for the interpretation. I have witnessed this pause many times in groups both as a participant and a leader. The monk rubbed his chin, and smiled.

"So that's why the washing machine broke!" The group's laughter knocked the nervousness out of me. I felt like a straight man in a comedy routine. Again!

"But," I stammered, "isn't there some Buddhist approach to dreams?" I asked this because I knew that Thây designs many training retreats specifically for therapists. Someone gave me a quick course in how all paradigms, ideas, and constructs are merely products of the mind and are all equal in their origin, all insignificant obstacles in the Dharma path to escape the endless cycle of birth and death.

Merik, a Scandinavian therapist, responded by saying that "sometimes a dream does have a key to some psychological issue, and sometimes it is no more than an image that occurs while we sleep." Another therapist, a Swede, nodded her head; I remembered a previous conversation with this woman, who was shocked that American therapists were not required to undergo psychoanalysis, a prerequisite for her degree.

"Well, then," I concluded, quoting Freud, "sometimes a cigar really *is* just a cigar." No fancy ideas here, just "Allez doucement, respirez et souriez," as the sign at the entrance said.

The Sangha's laughter warmed me more pleasantly than my intellectual probing. At one point, after a long walk to meet Ben, when I entered, laughing, with a companion, Ben commented to his friend, "My mother practices laughing meditation well!" I was really enjoying myself! This was becoming a real vacation instead of a mission to improve the mother-son relationship.

Soon it became common knowledge that I had had no film in the camera or cassettes in the recorder during our meeting with Thây. Later, when I tried to fax Thây to reschedule for pictures, the resident technical expert smiled and said that Thây would be very amused to hear that the camera had been empty of film, because he thinks the Sangha is more important than he is. On his tape *Call Me by My True Names*, after stating that the next Buddha who will come to us will be Maitreya, the Buddha of Love, he suggested that although the next Buddha could come as a person, she (sic!) could even appear in the form of a Sangha.

Subsequently, I spent the next few days photographing the residents, the visitors, the greenhouse that I had cleaned, the plum trees, the bookstore, the zendo, and especially, the compost pile, Plum Village's familiar symbol of the wheel of life. When I entered the bookstore to capture my memories, a monk, upon hearing my name, smiled broadly, took a pamphlet from the display that carried a picture of a rose, and immediately gave it to me. "For Ben's mother!" *A Rose for Your Pocket* was a ceremony that Thây had developed for Mother's Day after he learned about this American holiday, to encourage letter-writing and good communication with one's family. I sped-read the pamphlet to learn that this was the influence that motivated Ben to write his loving letter to me from his retreat and subsequently to send me many of Thây's tapes. Like a true Jewish mother, I became *farklempt*, blinking back my tear-duct attack.

The Sangha, however, provided one more moment of anxiety near the end of my stay. Before participating in a ceremony called "Beginning Anew," I was told that members of the Sangha were supposed to clarify things with one another. I was expecting a real comeuppance about my peculiar behavior on the Sabbath, or about my abrasive humor.

A slim white-haired woman in her young seventies began; she was the bride of the newlywed New Zealander in my first Dharma group.

"I want to water the flowers in Rosie," she said as she burst into hearty guffaws. I thought she was laughing at me. ". . . Because she always makes me laugh." The entire group joined in and laughed *with* me, who was speechless in surprise.

Others followed with more surprises.

One California flower child said, "I want to water the flowers in Rosie for having the courage to undertake this journey with her son." More *farklempt* behavior.

Merika summed up another characteristic. "I want to water the flowers in Rosie for the way she gets what she wants." This one brought the zendo down.

I was beginning to understand why devotees become devoted to the Sangha, but apparently, I didn't understand some of its basic operating rules. Later, when I was lost in thought, I bumped into Karl, Helga's husband, while the whole resident Sangha filed into a meeting. He had to stay outside, and so I imagined some wrong, some judgment, some managerial review board, and tried to offer some unwanted comforting words.

"You don't get it, do you?" Chagrined, this time I knew that I had committed a breach of etiquette.

"I guess I don't get it. Please explain."

"The idea here is, where can we be of the most use? Thây doesn't want people living here for more than four years; they should move on to the place where they can do the most good with their talents." So that's what the Sangha was discussing while we talked! I thought that he was excluded from the meeting for the wrong reasons, not for altruistic reasons. In fact, the Sangha had decided to return some of the nuns to Vietnam to help the people there. As our conversation became more animated and friendly and I could feel my old barriers drop, I confessed that I still couldn't reconcile the act of bowing with my own religion.

"You know," he said in his distinct German accent, "there's a book called *If You See the Buddha on the Road, Kill Him!* "

"Well, if you can arrange for that, then bowing won't be such a barrier!" Yes, I remembered this dog-eared book on my husband's bookshelf.

"Do you know that there is a Buddhist temple in Thailand that has no statue of Buddha, only a mirror? The monks bow to a mirror." I imagined the Torah scroll dressed in its traditional velvet in an ark lined with mirrors. That could even be theologically correct.

"Since G-d is faceless, our reflection might be the closest we come to seeing a manifestation," I replied as I thought of all the rabbinical literature on the biblical reference to being created "in the image of G-d."

A few days later when Karl's wife, Helga, sadly announced my departure, I remembered these amusing moments with her husband. I felt warmly toward them both when they sat on either side of me at my last meal in Plum Village. We also had a candid conversation about the swastika symbol on the Buddha. Had the wheel of Jewish-German relationship turned full circle in this beginning of a Holocaust healing for me?

We also discussed Thây's first visit to America. When they described how, during this visit, he had led an anti–Vietnam War march in New York in the sixties, another memory came back to me; it flowered when Helga invited me to say some parting words.

"I have learned a lot during my stay at Plum Village," I began. "I have learned about you, your past, and your Sangha, and I have also learned something about karma. I was just reminded of a time when Thây came to America to try to meet with the U.S. president, who relegated him to a lesser official. There was an anti-war march down the main streets of New York." Some diners looked startled at this reference to the war that was burned into their memory. I continued with a tug at my heart; perhaps this was a reminder of their own Asian Holocaust.

"I believe that Ben and I and my older daughter may have been in that march in New York City around the time of Thây's visit when he proposed his Five-Point Peace Proposal. I remember that we were in battalions of a hundred, and that we three were in the front row of one battalion. When we had to stop for a red light, some people on the curb started to scream: 'What kind of a mother are you!' 'Get those kids out of here!' Demonstrators ahead of us had red paint thrown at them. I put my arms around my children so that they would not think badly of themselves because of the bad names they were being called; I put myself between them and the hooligans. When all the other demonstrators noticed this, they began talking to my children, cheering them, and suddenly everyone around me was applauding them. Hundreds of people on the sidelines applauded until the end of the march when my children walked through two lines of applauding sympathizers."

The room became a gaggle of English and Vietnamese, gasps, exclamations, as the Vietnamese who didn't understand English urged the dewy-eyed nuns who did understand to translate. Soon the entire room was a rush of emotion.

"Just the other day," I continued, "I wondered why one of the kitchen nuns called me 'sister.' Maybe it has something to do with karma. What about karma? I have learned about karma here because, as I cared for you then, so now you cared for me during my stay. Now I have actually experienced it."

Translations in Vietnamese followed. Then they all rushed to me and warmly crowded around as Karl flashed my camera; the light bounced brightly around the white boards that lined the room. This, like the meeting with Thây, was also not to be captured in celluloid. The light was not right, but it is still bright and indelible in my memory and intertwined into my consciousness in ways that I would yet discover.

9

———◆———

Chicken Soup in Paris,
Challah in Kathmandu

I WELCOMED THE LONG TRAIN RIDE BACK TO PARIS TO
integrate the Plum Village events. That moment of sharing a cup
of tea with a Zen master felt like the experience between breaths,
steeped in the universal timeless pause of a beginning, middle, and
end all at once. Until we release from our animal body, experience
is our main reference; until we stop breathing, the main foundation of our experience is breath.

Like bumper stickers in my mind, pictures of Thây's sayings
prominently displayed in the bathrooms, near the mirrors, on the
backs of the doors of the toilet stalls, and in the hallways, punctuated my thoughts:

"Be part of the miraculous moment!"

"Please call me by my true names so that the doors of my heart
can be left open, the door of compassion."

The New Age emphasis on "the here and now" has certainly
been influenced by teachers like Thây, but some interpreters have

used this to rationalize total involvement in bodily pleasure. Ben at thirteen understood this misinterpretation, and his analysis of the present moment containing the future was integral to any experience of mysticism. Concentrating on our breath in the present can bring the experience of timelessness and the path to enlightenment to anyone who focuses on such a practice.

What was *my* true name? Was it the Vietnamese Nguyên Thông, the English Rosie, or the Jewish Rokheleh that my mother would call through the streets of my Canadian hometown? Can the soul, or what the Buddhists call our individual consciousness or our moment in being, which gets reborn again or enlightened, have a name? Or is it just an identity? Surely we all have a mission, a Work, whatever our beliefs, and perhaps that is our identity. But where is this written and how do we find it?

Thây says that all our experiences compose our being and that we must "hold, care, and transform." We should not "transform ourselves into a battlefield," for that would be dualistic and that is not Buddhism. We hold and take care of our feelings and experiences like a "mother taking care of a baby" to find out what is wrong, just as a mother analyzes the problem. We must look deeply into our pain, with mindfulness, and then that insight will transform and that will bring compassion. So our true name must be compassion and that must be the common source of being, something that I could identify as Divinity, the kind of Divinity that the Hasidic Jew addresses in prayer. In this context, prayer yearns for a union with G-d: in Hebrew, *devekut*, often translated as "cleaving." Thây has written that "the will of G-d is also our will, because we and G-d are one." This same conclusion was believed by the Jewish mystics.

Recalling Thây thumbing through the book I gave him, the *Tanya*, I wondered if he would read it. As we took the slow train to our express stop, I felt sad to leave him and my new friends. Shneur Zalman constantly referred to the soul's root in the common root of G-d. Chayyim Vital, a Kabbalist of the sixteenth and seventeenth centuries who lived in Safed, described in detail how the root of each soul is attached like a tree branch to the main tree and its roots; this is the Supreme Mind, or G-d. To access another person's being (soul), one must access one's own, and then compassion occurs. Surely there was some core similarity here between Judaism and Buddhism in the Interbeing that Thây describes.

Returning to Paris with these musings, Ben and I had a great smiling time comparing notes, first on the slow train, then on the bullet train, then shlepping through the stations, the Métro, and through the streets to Jane's kitchen. I hadn't enjoyed his company this thoroughly since reading to him as a very young boy the Time-Life science books that he devoured. Now the roles were reversed and it was Ben who was guiding me through the literature of experience. However, inevitably, Ben became weary of my slow walk, so he carried most of the luggage to walk quickly ahead of me and up to Jane's flat. He buzzed me into the entrance and called down to me from four flights of stairs, as I huffed and puffed my way up.

Something in Paris was different this time, something that went beyond smiles. It smelled like the stairway to my Aunt Becky the caterer's apartment that our family used to climb for our yearly Passover seder. I knew that I was always experiencing constant flashbacks—my consciousness could never stay in the moment without reminders—but this was uncanny. Jane greeted me like a long-lost relative and I loved it. Entering, I noticed a gift wrapped with ribbons on my daybed. It was for me. Jane had returned to the Jewish bookstore, where the owner decided with her that the book, *The Polish Jewry: History and Culture*, was meant for me. Jane had persuaded her to take a lower price (which she did not disclose to me). We had really adopted each other! It still makes me smile when I remember her face framed in the henna neon hair color then popular with Parisiennes.

The kitchen was warm with more surprises. I had given Jane a cookbook assembled by the parents at my grandson's Jewish day school, the Solomon Schechter School. She had read it in one night and produced some of its wonders, including the fabled source of Jewish penicillin itself, chicken soup. Like my aunt

Fania the agnostic from Krakow, Jane defined her Jewishness by her food. Gastronomy could become the new theology: Jewish chicken soup and Buddhist tea made a wonderful, hospitable meal. Dr. Abraham Maslow himself, the father of self-actualization psychology, was known to have said to his mother-in-law upon being served her chicken soup: "A good bowl of soup is as good as a poem."

I practiced the deep looking that Thây recommended. I believed that I saw Jane struggling with her metal canes down the Rue de Rosier, looking for the butcher and bargaining with him, at the greengrocer's collecting the vegetables, at the corner store collecting the noodles, and then shlepping these bags up the four flights of circular stairs. I saw her entering the hallway lined with antique nutcrackers and resting in a chair before she chopped and cooked and watched and stirred. This Jewish Buddhist *maydele* (young lady) had cooked a classic Jewish meal!

Later that night I struggled with sleep as the two old friends shared insights in the kitchen. Once again I opened Ben's prayer packet and placed my Hebrew prayerbook beside it; now they seemed like more comfortable traveling companions. Finally I felt sleepy enough to close both for the night. A surprising new lightness helped me to enter sleep with the memories of a great meal in the good company of my son and his Jewish friend.

Morning found us in the Orléans airport. After telling me again how Thây's poetic interpretation of Buddhism had been a good introduction to the more complex Vajrayana Tibetan Buddhism practiced in Nepal, Ben settled into his seat. For some reason, Air France had bumped us up to first class from economy class for the flight to New Delhi airport. Here each seat was larger and more comfortable. I had never traveled in such luxury in my life, nor had my son, the world traveler. With individual TV screens for each seat and five movie choices, Ben, who had been a movie buff before his retreat, now made up for lost time and, instead of sleeping, watched all five movie options while I enjoyed the simple pleasures of extra leg room with more comfort for sleeping. Also, the food was better and more abundant. Hearing English spoken with a French accent made me feel very cosmopolitan. "Madame Ros-*en*-zweig with ze kosh-*er* meal?"

We had time to catch up, and Ben checked to make sure that I had antimalaria medication and had gotten my gamma-globulin shots; moreover, in an interesting role reversal, he almost spoon-fed me his herbal echinacea solution as a protection against illness. The nurse in the traveler's clinic back home had questioned these extra precautions, and I repeatedly told her that my son was a seasoned traveler who knew about these things. Besides, he would not want a sick mother on his hands; that would cause more complications.

When the pilot announced that we would soon land in New Delhi, I had no idea what to expect next. As the plane began its descent, we appeared to enter a layer of dust. Disembarking, we walked through smog to enter the airport's holding zones. Everyone seemed to be smoking, and the air reflected it. Ben told me that there were no airline desks but that the ticket agent would find us.

"But how do they know who we are?" I asked.

"Somehow they know," he assured me. "Ticket agents roam around and inquire until they find their assigned passengers. Don't worry, the system somehow works." We did become anxious, however, when we thought that we would not be able to sit and guard our luggage. Ben had repeatedly warned me how notorious India's big cities were for clever thieves. I got edgy when we passed by the military personnel guarding all the exits and entrances and someone sneaked by us and whispered, "Have cigarettes?" I looked blankly at his semishaven face as he pointed to his cigarette and said, "Have tobacco like this?" I looked away and played dumb.

Ben paced around until the agent found us. We would be allowed to watch our luggage, but the distance we needed to carry it to the lounge made us both worry. Our next problem was getting the luggage, our porters, and the luggage trolleys into a small elevator, but I couldn't understand the gabble of Hindi and pidgin English that tried to solve the problem. Ben demonstrated skill at speaking slowly in simple English to get us through this barrier and parked on some long sofas in the double-ballroom-size lounge. The idea was to reserve enough space for us to stretch out and sleep (we were here for the night!) and still watch our own luggage.

My drowsiness pulled me into small cat naps until I was startled awake by the fascinating parade strolling by: women in saris or Punjabi suits consisting of loose pants under a long tunic, men in turbans, Germans in stylish Western clothes, Caucasians in Eastern clothes, fashionable French women, and American as well as European hippies. I hadn't had such a good time people-watching since my honeymoon in New York when, at eighteen, I had my first big excursion out of my small Canadian birthplace, to the big city. Only the New York subway with its varieties of human forms and dress codes could match this, but then again, with its homeless people living on the street, New York City sometimes resembled an impoverished Asian metropolis. However, here in India, the smog inside the airport reflected these travelers' fondness for smoking—not my usual preferred environment. My fatigue reminded me that we had an eleven-hour wait, from midnight to almost noon the next day.

Did I doze and dream, or did I daydream the memory of that constant black cloud of coal smoke that haunted our small apartment in the little border town in Windsor, Ontario, when I was a preschooler? My poor mother always had trouble with the furnace, so the walls were once again dusty as we sat at dinner. I couldn't understand my parents' dramatic Yiddish conversation, but my teenaged siblings did. Born in Poland, they had been without a father when he left for America during their early childhood, to work and save money for their passage; they always joined the family discussion with the usual hysterical simultaneous shouting. This was the day that my mother realized that only she and perhaps one other sister in her family of more than eighty people, having emigrated well before the beginning of the war, had escaped the era of "the camps." Silence hung like a cloud of guilt on our family's consciousness for leaving our relatives to their terrible fate. I was in my forties when I first learned of their fate at Auschwitz. Later, when I read the Nelly Sachs poem on the camps that begins, "oh the chimneys," this brought me a different kind of coal dust, one that continually seeps into my dreams. Even now, when I dote on my grandchildren, I wonder: What would it have been like to have had grandparents?

Startled, I sat up in the airport sofa, unnerved at these reminders of my immigrant family. I squinted to see a crowd of European tourists, chattering, animated (in the middle of the night!)—and smoking! Their German accents cut through my reveries; a canceled Lufthansa flight left these wayfarers stranded. Oh how our karma returns to present new opportunities for growth. This was not the nineteen-forties, and German accents were no longer signs of danger. I tried to remember Thich Nath Hanh's caution not to mistake a rope for a snake—his favorite example of erroneous perception—or the Buddhist wheel of teaching for a Nazi swastika. Warmed by my memories of Helga and Karl, I watched these tourists walk through the terminal to board another flight.

Meanwhile, poor sleepless Ben had been walking up and down the long length of this lounge. Back home prior to this, he would often narrate stories about this terminal and his fears of having his luggage stolen. If he hadn't taken the responsibility for all the travel details, I would probably be worrying in his place. However, I would have been too overwhelmed by hearing stories of Indian poverty to ever travel here on my own. Again I felt that sympathetic paralyzing knot in my stomach as I remembered pictures of hundreds of hands outstretched from emaciated bodies.

However, now I needed Ben to guard the luggage, as an urgent need overpowered my dread of the Indian restrooms. With my toiletries, I walked behind the large metal partition with the sign for women clearly marked. Two emaciated petite women, body and hair draped in maroon gauze saris, approached with one hand open and the other pointing to rough paper in a pile near the sinks, saying, "American dollars?" Were they beggars? Attendants? Untouchables? I avoided their gaze, walked to the nearest stall, and closed the door. Third World plumbing confronted me in the form of a hole in the tiled floor. A faucet to the left of this dripped near an empty pitcher. That's why they were selling toilet paper! Clumsy, groggy from sleep, with an aching knee and a bad sense of balance, I thanked all my experience hiking in the woods during my children's teenage years when I packed my own toilet paper. Now, stationed at the sink, the women tried to sell me toilet paper again! To wash my hands? I tried to say, "No, thank you," persistently and insistently. Finally I waved my own Handi-wipes at them until they retreated to their corner, where they sat on their haunches.

"I've been initiated into Asian culture," I said to Ben as he rose to take his walk again.

Even though we had packed fruit and canned tuna fish, he still wanted to tour the food stalls. He reminded me not to drink the water or eat anything that needed washing. I ate a banana and an orange, both fruits protected by their skins. Finally, a Royal Nepal Airlines representative found us and took us to board a small plane with propellers for a short, skillful flight over the Himalayan range to the Kathmandu valley. As the pilot began a quick intense descent, the clouds opened briefly for a quick view of the snowcapped Himalayas; my eyes widened to see my first glimpse of the countryside. We saw the green terraces civilizing and cultivating the mountains with rice fields and yellow mustard plantings, Nepal's main source for cooking oil. The pilot favored sharp curves in his circle down, even though my stomach disagreed. We saw brick factories pouring dark smoke from their chimneys. Close by, the landscape was a mix of lush cultivation, fancy houses, and crumbling poorer structures. Remembering a more rural village atmosphere, Ben felt disappointed to see the growing land development and the loss of greenery. We began quicker descent to the Kathmandu Airport, the entrance to the Shangri-la of *Lost Horizon*, that Himalayan utopia that my husband had romanticized. How ironic that his health had kept him at home and that I, the reluctant cynic, was now landing here instead of him.

Disembarking after a twelve-hour stopover in New Delhi onto
a windy tarmac with small planes buzzing by added to my bone-
weary confusion; my fatigue discombobulated me now. An old
bus, with the seats positioned lengthwise like a World War II
bomber plane, approached; we all boarded courteously and
calmly, filling every available crevice with our bodies. The terminal was a crowded, dark building whose passengers were an international mix of costume, language, and skin color, all moving
in their own ethnic shorthand of walk and talk. Inside, a line of
yellow baggage carts wound out to greet us—or perhaps they
weren't moving and I was only dizzy. Quickly and deftly my fellow passengers hooked them all until I was left, clumsy and
empty-handed. Finally Ben caught one and skillfully wheeled it
next to a moving assembly line that promised us our luggage.
Overheated from the closeness of the crowding queue, I zipped
my coat around my hips and crashed down, straddling the end of
the cart like a weary woman cowboy.

A gaggle of dark-skinned beauties in colorful saris looked at
me, looked at one another, and giggled en masse. Oy vey, another
breach of manners! Embarrassed, I smiled and turned back to sit
in a side-saddle position. Dressed in a mustard Punjabi, a petite,
round-faced Indian woman with short-cropped dark hair and
glasses maneuvered herself beside me. Still conditioned to hearing
English with either a French or a Vietnamese accent, I slowly ad-
justed to the musical accent of India as she introduced herself. She
was curious about us, a strapping young man with auburn hair
and glasses and an intellectual face, and this stout middle-aged
woman. I apologized for my indiscretion while Ben controlled
his embarrassment. I had received no prior instructions for this
situation. In a flashback to Plum Village, I remembered Karl's
joking about older women with younger men after I identified
myself as this handsome man's mother. After all, that was the
South of France.

"This is my son, Ben," I immediately informed my new friend,
Promila.

"What do you do?" Her direct approach reminded me of a

news-gathering reporter. Poor Ben, with his career then unde-cided, told her he was in computers. This was true; at home he was always at my computer learning, advising, using e-mail.

"You must save your money, you know, so that your mother doesn't have to keep supporting you." Ben and I laughed at her instructions. I tried to tell her that his parents had long ago stopped supporting him financially. However, our new friend did not hear me. Lecturing my son on his filial responsibilities to me and to himself, she continued on.

"Excuse me," I said, interrupting her, "but I believe those are *my* lines." Our idioms seemed to miss each other. I became the de-scription that a Plum Village friend had bestowed on me: "the typical overprotective Jewish mother."

"I have worked in computers which are here in Nepal," said Ben, "and that are used on Wall Street in America." Instead of saying, "I've done computers here and at home," he was imitat-ing the "weird English" that he believed Asians would understand better. Many Indians speak a proper Queen's English full of the music of Indian intonations, without contractions, with an overemphasis on infinitives and long dependent clauses. This pre-cise grammatical usage is still a sign of the upper class in India.

Satisfied with Ben's replies, she began questioning me about what I did. I replied that I was writing a book about my meetings with Buddhist teachers from Vietnam and Tibet. A light went off in this little lady's face. Her friends, dressed in bright, amazing colors skillfully wrapped around their bodies, watched us atten-tively with their brown beautiful eyes. I wondered how all that fabric stayed in place so well.

Promila launched into an explanation of herself and her mis-sion to Kathmandu. She explained that she was a delegate to the Public Service International's South Asian Regional Seminar on Women's Trade Union Rights. She was in her thirties and refused to marry anyone her father selected because she would only marry someone of her own choosing. Promila knew that confes-sion in conversation leads to reciprocal disclosure from strangers. After realizing that Ben was my son, she had at once uncovered all the necessary information to form an opinion of the two of us. When she learned that I was a writer, she immediately invited me to cover the conference as a Western woman journalist. Then she turned to Ben and began to instruct him again to carve out a future for himself, get a wife, save his money, and stop being a burden on his mother's finances.

I informed her that Ben, at thirty-three, had been self-sufficient for a long time, had saved his money, and was now planning for the next phase of his life—after of course, consulting with his guru. I told her that I was confident that whatever he did would be successful. Realizing that this was too much English for her to digest, Ben just told her again that he worked in the computer field.

"Perhaps *you* can come to our conference as a journalist and write about us." Ben liked the idea; free of the responsibilities of worrying about me and my stamina, he could wander about freely and look for his old friends. Promila continued her invitation. "The PSI is having a South Asian Regional Seminar on Women's Trade Union Rights; I am officially inviting you to join us; we are coming together from India, Bangladesh, Sri Lanka, Pakistan, and, of course, Nepal." Receiving so formal an invitation, I stood almost at attention. She wrote all the details in my notebook. "So I hope to see you when you come to the Woman's Seminar at the Marco Polo Business Hotel." Satisfied, she turned to me to give the directions to her hotel. All the saris, after the events were translated for them, waved a smiling good-bye to us and slowly encouraged me, in their high English-Indian dialect, to attend.

When the luggage arrived, everyone made a dash for the conveyer belt. I caught one bag while Ben deftly scooped up the remaining three. Immediately he wheeled our cart quickly toward the customs line as I rushed to follow. The few Westerners were all dressed like us, in hiking clothes. I was a far cry from the well-dressed French businesswomen who had eyed us disdainfully on the bullet train from Paris. Ben led me quickly through customs, parked me with the luggage, and left to hire a taxi. Never, he cautioned, never go out of the terminal with your luggage to look for a cab. Always get your cab reserved inside the terminal before you leave the building. I soon realized how wise he was. As we wheeled our luggage outside to the designated cab, suddenly half a dozen young Nepalese surrounded to help us carry or at least touch each bag.

"Try not to talk to them, Mom," instructed Ben as he wheeled our gear single-mindedly toward the cab. I was told to get into the cab while the driver and Ben loaded up. Every one of these young entrepreneurs simultaneously sang the refrain that I would hear everywhere: "Rupee, rupee."

The dusty drive into Kathmandu along the unpaved roads full of potholes jostled us. We passed the walled enclaves of the diplomatic offices and expensive hotels, side-by-side shops with clothes hanging outside their windows lining the sides of buildings, above them outdoor displays of fruit and meat with flies buzzing, and scores of signs. The signs advertised their shop's fares in English, Nepali, and even Hebrew (evidently to attract Israeli trekkers): "Pharmacy," "Ayurvedic Massage," "Trekking Company."

Many shops displayed thangkas, pictures artistically painted on fabric framed in silk, waving slowly in the heat; some represented the Buddhist wheel of life, mandalas for meditation, or a human form with its chakras, or subtle energy points, brightly highlighted. Ben continually marveled at the proliferation of buildings since his last visit several years ago; where once rice paddies reflected the sky, now new two-story brick homes housed large families with their servants. We passed outside the walled park of the royal palace with its beggars like skeletons seated on wheeled platforms with their powdered limbs. Schoolchildren dressed in their matching school blazers with pants or skirts casually walked by without a glance at these sights. Ben commented that the local crime syndicate reportedly assigns these busy waystations to favored beggars for a piece of the action; he said that some beggars actually become quite wealthy by Nepalese standards.

During the cab ride, I received my first lesson in Nepali with the phrase *saano paisaa chhai na,* which means, "I have no small change." Ben demonstrated how to make my head motion agreeably form the letter *S.* Saying "yes" or "no" depended on the smile on my face. He taught me quickly about Nepalese bargaining techniques. I must adhere to the ultimate rule: "Always allow the shopkeeper to save face." Also I must know that the shopkeeper will sell at a loss to maintain a civil relationship with the customer. This was beginning to sound like the Ten Commandments of street shopping. Ben said that Israelis were disliked here because they were unaware of this rule or took advantage of it. Apparently, Israeli tourists were known to browbeat the merchants into loss; as a result they were often asked to leave a stall upon entering. Coincidentally, back home my husband and I had just begun a Talmud study group with a discussion of the ethical practices classified under the heading of *ona'ah.* Some translators render this Hebrew word as "cheating," "fraud," or "deception," but I like Rabbi Adin Steinsaltz's interpretation based on the word's Hebrew root, meaning to cause distress or suffering. The rabbis of the Talmud forbade entering a shop and asking the price of any goods that one does not intend to buy, because that would cause suffering to the shopkeeper.

We entered the neighborhood called Thamel, where the smog hung in the air like a black soot of coal dust dirtying everything. Again! The main shopping area with shops tightly packed amid narrow streets, speeding cars spitting black smoke, bicycle rickshaws pulled by thin drivers pumping madly, and motorcycles with drivers in black leather jackets, helmets, and bare-headed women in saris sitting side-saddle on the back; pedestrians had to hop quickly onto the narrow curves to protect their own safety. We saw some men in native Nepalese dress with slim pants, long Nehru jacket, and narrow peaked hat, while others wore Western-style suits; and then there were Westerners trying to dress like Nepalese. Ben told me about "Freak Street," named for the droves of hippies who invaded Nepal in the hope of quick enlightenment and cheap hashish.

Finally, we turned a corner into a less traveled lane with its newly repainted stupa overlooking a trash-littered street, gutters flowing with feces, and cows walking and mooing freely. Our cab drove through an iron gate along a quiet, long walled driveway, bringing us to a white four-story hotel with terraces, an outdoor restaurant, a long white lobby with maroon sofas, and the welcome desk under a large wooden carved peacock. With Nepalese television news blaring in the background, a smiling, attractive desk clerk in Western clothes welcomed us to the Hotel Shakti. Five dollars a night (which Ben had reduced to $4.30 because of our extended stay) for a private room with a shared bath.

We walked up to the third floor, through outdoor terraces, to our two rooms; mine was a corner room overlooking the mountains and numerous large TV satellite dishes on all the neighbors' roofs. We would share the bath with one other room; it was a long tiled room with a drain, a sink, a Western toilet (finally), and a showerhead; there was no partition between these functions. Sometimes this entire room would resemble the wet dripping walls of what my father used to call the *shvizt*—the steamroom where immigrants assembled for their weekly pre-Sabbath bath on the Lower East Side in New York.

This was to be home for the next three weeks in Shangri-la. Thankfully we ordered room service for hot steaming lemon tea, cheese sandwiches, and fruit. It was Friday evening, and I unpacked the challah, the braided Sabbath bread, purchased at a Jewish bakery before we left Paris. I lit candles without the hassle of explanations, and blessed my son that he should keep the faith like Ephraim and Manasseh. Jewish mothers habitually say their most heartfelt prayers after the candle-lighting blessing, so I thanked G-d for a safe journey and asked for protection against all that might befall us in this strange new place that was so familiar to my son.

10

Jewish Karma

I AROSE TO RELAX INTO MY SABBATH MORNING PRAYERS and weekly Torah portion reading, which was Exodus 30:11 to 34:35. This vividly describes the punishment for building the golden calf, a mistaken god-image to worship in the desert while Moses was receiving the Ten Commandments on Mount Sinai. The Sabbath Torah portion pointed to one of the unresolved issues of the day. Today as I was struggling with the Jewish antipathy to idols in a Hindu country with icons everywhere, Ben told me that we were to meet a real idol-maker. Later that morning I entered the hotel dining room and saw Ben with a muscular, tall Tibetan. I was introduced to Lama Norlha's cousin, an idol-builder, who was to use the lama's gift of gold to create a small golden replica of the Buddha. Sometimes I feel that there are no accidents, only reminders of recurrent past individual or ancestral actions. Since the translation of *karma* is "intentional action," I was intrigued with this seemingly random juxtaposition of the day's Torah portion and the breakfast conversation.

I was also reminded of Shakespeare's oft-quoted Shylock

speech, so appropriate when Jews are treated like "the other." Shylock says, "I am a Jew . . . hath not a Jew hands, organs, dimensions, senses, affections, passions?" Perhaps, I thought, I should apply it to this situation, where I was thinking about Ben's friend as an "other." (Later that week, we were invited to the lama's cousin's house and met his family. I saw how he honored his mother by having her live with them, and he seemed like a nice, hospitable man. Upon leaving his house I thought to myself: Hath not an idol-maker, senses, affections, passions?)

That Shabbat's Torah portion had inspired numerous rabbinical commentaries relating how the women had refused to contribute their gold earrings and rings to build the idol. Women were described as having special insight. I recalled hearing the late Lubavitcher Rebbe's talk in the mid-eighties explaining that, as a reward, the Torah was really given to women first before the men, and how, fittingly, they should be given the task of being teachers to their children. In addition, the monthly observance of Rosh Chodesh (the first day of the lunar month) was made a special holiday for women.

Another part of the day's agenda was a walk to meet Promila and her sister delegates at the women's conference at the Marco Polo Hotel. What special insight might Asian women have, and how would I learn about it?

When I told Ben that I wouldn't travel by car on the Sabbath and wanted to walk to the women's seminar, he was glad to have a respite from his responsibilities as tour guide to his unschooled Jewish mother. After scheduling a future visit to Lama Norlha's cousin's family, he led me to the Marco Polo Business Hotel and the waiting arms of my Indian hostess.

Promila introduced us to the conference delegates from India, Nepal, Bangladesh, Sri Lanka, and Pakistan. The organizer, Jay Bahn, the only other man present, kept addressing all comments to Ben throughout the introductions until Promila informed him who the journalist was. After much teasing from the women, Jay-Bahn, as he was called, began to give me pamphlets, press releases, a keychain with a very graphic cartoon of sexual exploitation in the workplace, and the delegate's information package. Everyone continued to greet me in their native language, bowing and shaking hands. I couldn't catch one word in any language because even the English sounded foreign to me.

The Pakistani delegate, a young computer maven with gorgeous dark eyes, bowed and said, "Salaam aleikum." Now here were some words that sounded familiar. When I responded with "Shalom aleichem" in Hebrew, the eyes shifted from left to right. A rather chilly pale descended around me, and I hoped I hadn't started something I couldn't handle. I recalled reading disturbing reports of international anti-Semitism at the United Nations Women's Decade Conferences in Mexico City, Copenhagen, and Nairobi in Letty Cottin Pogrebin's book *Deborah, Golda, and Me: Being Female and Jewish in America*. Quickly I left, wondering whether I should return.

As we walked away, Ben advised me not to emphasize my Jewish identity. "In this part of the world, Mom, they will first identify you as an American. They probably have never seen a Jew before. If they like you and then find out you're also Jewish, then they will have a favorable impression of Jews, because you will represent that for them." Pondering this advice, I went upstairs to nap, while he walked toward Thamel with an anticipatory bounce in his step.

During the next few days, I often remembered Ben's words during my time with these exotic women and their male organizer, a handsome, svelte man, whose daily summary of the proceedings seemed directed to me. He projected the zeal and charisma of union organizers in the early stages of their mission: people like Cesar Chavez rallying the migrant agricultural workers, and the organizers of the early International Ladies' Garment Workers. I remembered Pete Seeger singing all those old union songs, and I thought of my great-aunt Zelda, who was involved with the Workman's Circle, and her colleague Emma Goldman. These Asian women delivered report after report of sexual abuse and exploitation. One nurse from Sri Lanka reported that women after childbirth were "willingly by the doctors left to die" because of the inconvenience of saving them. The sessions included how to use the union and the law, how to write reports, and some experiential exercises imported from our American New Age movement. I thought I was back in my decade of corporate human resource training, or, even earlier, the days when I first experienced the problem-solving techniques of the early encounter groups. I was led through a "trust walk" where, blindfolded, I submitted to an unknown guide who steered me around the landscape. I watched my new woman friends, with silk scarves over their eyes, allowing themselves to be led around improvised obstacles to learn about their inner resistance. These exercises were similar to the ones I first knew in the late 60s at the Esalen Institute in California. My familiarity with what they were experiencing gave me a feeling of closeness to these women, and I offered my extra sweater to some in the overly air-conditioned chill of the hotel meeting room.

Throughout all this, Promila kept looking at me affectionately. One day she invited me to the delegates' lunchroom because we had become quite close. She volunteered to read my palm, and her conclusions were uncanny.

"You are given to much self-introspection that could lead to deep depression. Only your faith in G-d will keep you from falling into these bouts with yourself. Also, if you were not married, you would probably be a nun."

"During my adolescence," I exclaimed, "I dreamed of being a nun, writing alone in an ivory tower. That, however, was quite impossible because Jews do not have nunneries."

"You are Jewish?" she said, putting down her fork and looking into my eyes. "You are changing my opinion of Jews. Do you know it has been said that the twenty-five million Jews were killed in the war because of the karma that all the money-lending brought about?"

Because of my previous two-week meditation retreat, I heard her startling words going through my ears like curiously new unattached words. Thich Nhat Hanh had cautioned against mistaking a rope for a snake. I sat with my eyes wide and my mouth open, trying to practice his "deep listening" with compassion. I seemed to be unable to locate any emotion, only the detached feeling of a researcher in some unknown archive of history.

"It was six million," I said calmly, reviewing my son's meditation instructions en route, "and I do remember hearing about this karma." Twenty years ago, I had heard a lecture that ascribed the Holocaust's karmic cause to the way Jews treated their non-Jewish neighbors, but my own family's large and painful loss at Auschwitz made me dismiss the lecturer's comment. In the impassioned letter I had sent Ben during his retreat, I had urged him to promise never to forget my family, as a basis for continuing our heritage; he hadn't respond favorably to my prodding. I dismissed this memory and focused on my conversation with Promila. "Besides," I continued, "very few Jews are money-lenders now; most are in other fields. Jews went into these mercantile fields in the Middle Ages because of many governments' restrictions forbidding them to pursue more conventional work. The occupation of merchant or trader became one of the possibilities. Because of persecution and restrictions on trade and habitation, the Jewish tradesman was seen as a 'wandering Jew.' As a merchant, he could use his contacts in other places to bring goods from one area to another, much as the Sherpas of Nepal do today. However, there are rules about business practices, rabbinically decreed, that are based on compassion."

"Then I must rethink this," Promila replied. Later some incidents made me conclude that word of this conversation got around.

That afternoon included a fiery speech from the organizer describing incidents of young daughters seduced into a life of prostitution by some self-appointed religious leader, and more reports on women's conditions in each country. Surprisingly, I was then asked to address the delegates about my own life. I told them that I felt I was watching history in the making. Gathering zest, I narrated Great-Aunt Zelda's story about coming to America at the turn of the century, leaving behind a loveless arranged marriage, becoming active in the International Ladies' Garment Workers

Union, and joining a utopian village with another Jewish woman, Emma Goldman. I explained Emma Goldman's historic role in the unions. I told them about the injustices committed against the garment workers and the 1911 Triangle Waist Company fire that took the lives of many Jewish women. The owners had the factory doors locked to protect against stealing. It had a strong impact on Eastern European Jews, most of whom had lost a friend, relative, or acquaintance, or had even been employed by Triangle at one time or another. It was a Jewish woman organizer's speech that turned the tide in the union's support. By comparing the fire to the Spanish Inquisition of Jews, she enlisted the support of uptown Jewry for the union. I told them how this history had played itself out in my family with my role model, Zelda.

Afterward, my new friends asked me to pose for many pictures with them. Later, during a seminar outing, my friend from Bangladesh sang "We Shall Overcome" to a bongo beat. That young Muslim beauty from Pakistan, who had greeted me earlier with her "Salaam aleikum," came closer to us, asked for my blessing, and put her head on my shoulder.

"Mama," she said (everyone in Asia who was younger than me called me Mama), "I love you. I have so much respect for your people." She took off her earrings. "You like this? I give it to you." Since I had missed her dance the night before because of a bronchial illness, she performed it again with all the insinuations of a harem maid. She kept giggling at my son, who decided to come along for a day trip to the shrines in Bhaktapur. I told her that she reminded me of my youngest daughter, who had become very religious and subsequently received twenty-two marriage proposals.

"Oh, Mama," she giggled, pulling her veil over her face, "I have received twenty-eight!" Ben and I couldn't stop laughing as she, racing for the bus in her golden high heels, stumbled in the mud and "accidentally" fell against him.

Subsequently, I overheard Ben describing my union adventures to his Tibetan friends; he also commented that one of the delegates had asked him how his Buddhism conjoined with his Jewish heritage. Ben had been speaking half Nepali and half English, so I couldn't quite follow the conversation. I finally had the nerve to ask him whether he considered himself Jewish.

"Of course," he replied, sending a smile across my face. "I have a Jewish mother, don't I?" He's a charmer, my son.

My Jewish Buddhist son had become my guru on Asian diplomacy. By correctly advising me about the Asian mentality during the women's conference, he had my best interests at heart. He was not surprised when I later reported how the ladies' opinion about karma had turned because of his advice. He was also becoming a diplomat with his Jewish mother.

11

Meeting the Root Guru

EVEN THOUGH I MANAGED TO ATTEND THE WOMEN'S seminar, I had become ill with respiratory congestion in my trachea. With eyes tearing, voice hoarse, and a continual feeling of dizziness, I unexpectedly vomited in the streets in front of a pharmacy. Ben ran inside to buy medication and led me to a nearby restaurant, where he directed me to sit down for hot tea and lemon. Illness, according to the Tibetan medicine practiced by monks, is caused by ignorance, excess, and life-style. This version of Asian healing is a marriage of religion, traditional medical practices, and folk remedies. Traveling in exotic landscapes certainly made encounters with such remedies likely. However, Ben thought Western medicine was better for immediate relief, so we found an outpost with a large red cross painted on the shingle, and bought into the higher-priced cure. The doctor, a Nepali graduate of a "two-year Canadian medical school" (was there such a thing?), prescribed a very strong antibiotic in spite of my reported history of allergies to penicillin. It killed my congestion along with my energy and created a large body rash that this doctor diagnosed as bed bugs or possibly a reaction to the soap that the chambermaids used to wash the hotel sheets. I wonder what I would have learned about myself had I gone to a Buddhist medical practitioner who could ferret out the karmic cause of my stifled breath.

Dreams returned to my sleep and pictured me cleaning the streets of garbage and my vomit; I accidentally kept dropping debris everywhere. Suddenly, like an edict from heaven, lightning bolts extended spidery veins, lighting the sky, penetrating the ground, and surrounding me. Somehow, I was not the source of this light but the cause of it. This brightness spewed forth a newborn little golden calf that came toward me and frightened me. I awoke and calmed myself with the thought that I had no real need to fear because I didn't believe in false images. However, a biblical image floated through my consciousness: the earth opening up to swallow the Israelites for their creation of a false image, a golden calf.

This bright morning, my son announced that we were going to see his "root guru" later today. Over breakfast Ben gave me a thumbnail history of Nepal, home of the sacred Himalaya, the roof of the world, where, at Lumbini in the western plains, Gautama Buddha was born some twenty-five hundred years ago; today Buddhism and Hinduism coexist as friends in this Hindu kingdom. In fact there is a lot of borrowing of each from the other.

At present, some twenty-two million people live in Nepal, over five hundred thousand in Kathmandu alone, and perhaps three times that many in the valley. From the low valleys to the highest Himalayas, with as many as fifty distinct languages and dialects, it is a land of diversity. Yet I couldn't find one synagogue in all my searchings. (I later learned that Lubavitcher Hasidim fly to Kathmandu every year to conduct a Passover seder for about three hundred people at the Israeli embassy.)

While Ben recounted the history and mythology, my mind kept sticking on certain facts that attracted me. I remembered that Ben can be equally thorough when describing a movie he loves. Very often I don't have to see it after hearing the details of the plot from Ben, but it takes me a little while to integrate all the details.

"So Buddha," I began.

"Shakyamuni Buddha, Mom."

"Okay, Shakyamuni Buddha," I continued, "wasn't he born in India into wealth and protected?"

"Well, it was India then, but now it's in the Terai, the southern part of Nepal. When Shakyamuni Buddha realized that no one can escape sickness, old age, and death, and that life is suffering, he set out to solve the problem of relief from suffering. When he became enlightened, he taught the Eightfold Path."

"So if Buddhism started here, and now that this has become a Tibetan center, wouldn't it make sense for the hidden valleys here to house Shangri-la instead of the valleys north of Tibet? Myths have been refashioned before. Remember the movie *Lost Horizon* that our family saw so many times?"

"You know that movie was filmed in Ojai, California," he chuckled. "Shangri-la, or Shambhala in Sanskrit, is a legendary kingdom in the Himalayas, described in a tantric text called the *Kalachakra*. Its king became enlightened, and then his whole kingdom became enlightened and vanished into a nonphysical realm."

"But wouldn't it be nice if Shangri-la really existed somewhere in these valleys?"

"Mom, Shambhala is a celestial kingdom, not a literal place. It's only attainable in the spiritual sense, as the state of awakened consciousness that exists within everyone."

"I still think that if a community works toward utopia, it's always possible to realize Shangri-la here on earth."

"Okay, Mom, have it your way." Just as I was armed to tease him further, I hadn't expected this. Somehow Ben's humoring me turned into another laughing meditation. He was now teasing *me*.

Having explored Nepal's past through my son's account, I could now venture forth into the present. Walking by the Royal Palace, we witnessed the rhythmic maneuvers of Gurkhas as they sometimes spilled into the streets to strut, jog, or walk beside us.

We stopped by the carpet shop belonging to Ben's old friend K.P., who once owned the only carpet shop in town. Ben showed me where he used to sleep on the floor when he and his friend were less affluent. Now there were scores of carpet shops, and K.P. owned a carpet factory where he produced original boutique designs sold in Europe. Unaccustomed to the narrow roads and the speeding traffic, I barely noticed a speeding motor rickshaw when Ben pulled me against the building to avoid a collision. My constant gaping at exotic and interesting people, places, and things became almost dangerous more than once.

In one shop that manufactured fabric purses, I witnessed Ben bargain as he had instructed me. He swayed his head with a smile, very subtly indicating agreement or disagreement, but always smiling. This was not the intense bargaining and arguing in the Arab *shuk*, or shopping bazaar, in Jerusalem. At one point Ben read the eyes of the merchant and decided to stop driving the price down, because it might make the merchant lose money. So Ben was following the talmudic principles on *ona'ah*. I wish I could take credit for this, but the truth is that once we have an adult child over thirty, he has spent plenty of time away from home learning how to become himself. I once learned this from Ben himself when I apologized for the grief of his childhood, for his witnessing of parental arguments and sometimes feeling unstable about the family. He told me that was in the past and that he had left it there; he alleviated the guilt of the Jewish mother who believes she determines her child's future by her present behavior. The future belongs to our children, and sometimes we have no influence on their direction. However, if we are lucky, they will bring it to us—if we can handle it.

Next, we visited the shop of another friend's father, where I proceeded to buy hats and a vest of Tibetan design. I was going to give the hats away as yarmulkes. Finally, we had lunch in K.C.'s Restaurant, where Ben considered the salads safe enough to eat; here they soaked the vegetables in iodine and then rewashed them. A lover of greens, I hadn't crunched any in weeks and made up for this deprivation quickly.

Now it was time to go to Boudhanath, the home of Ben's guru and the largest enclave of Tibetans from Nepal, twelve thousand in number. The cab drove east through less densely populated streets until we came to the entrance to the area. The walkways and roads did not allow access to cars, so we walked up past stalls and clothing for sale hanging on poles. Ahead of us was a stupa, a moundlike reliquary with a huge dome mounted on a series of terraces. On its square spire were two large painted eyes, a long OM sign for a nose, and a tall pointed roof for a crown, hung with strings of prayer flags. Under the eyes, one set for each direction of the compass, was the round white dome painted with golden semicircles. I saw a worker tossing the golden-colored water in arcs, achieving the same even pattern each time. No mistakes here. The base held 108 images of the Buddha and 147 prayer wheels, according to my guidebook. Occasionally devotees walked by twirling the wheels, cylinder-shaped objects that rotate on a stick, containing written mantras and other prayers. By virtue of the metaphor of turning the "wheel of Dharma," in spinning the prayer wheel it's as if one is having the Dharma taught. Devotees touched the wheels going and coming from these sacred sites as automatically as Jews touch the mezuzahs on their doorposts.

We walked up a slight incline by a circle of beige houses. Ben said that some of them were monasteries, some hotels, and others private residences. Entering a courtyard, we walked toward a set of white stairs that we climbed to enter another inner courtyard. A band of dogs grazed on some discarded food. Here was a large multistoried white building flanked by two wings with each tiled roof terraced back.

Here I saw the place that had first sparked Ben's serious interest in Buddhism. Travelers like him often come to the court of a guru, but when Ben's Boolean logic challenged Chökyi Nyima with many questions, the Rinpoche ("Precious Teacher") answered everything with good humor, charm, and intelligence. The turning point, Ben recalled, came early with Rinpoche's teasing response, "Ah, so we have a scientist in our midst!" Laughter and affection ensued as every challenge was eventually met.

We walked into a small innermost courtyard and were about to enter a door in the back corner of this maze when a young monk in maroon robes lugging laundry bags, who appeared to be a preteen, saw Ben, dropped his bundle, and ran into the building. "It's Ben!" he shouted loudly and happily. "Ben is back! Ben is back!" He carried the news as he raced through the labyrinth, echoing my son's name over and over again. We walked past a large shrine room full of large Buddhas and up four flights of stairs to a large foyer, where we parked our shoes. An attendant came out, and his face brightened when he saw Ben; he slipped behind a curtained entrance to announce him. We entered another shrine room lined with golden statues of the Buddha. A Tibetan with handsome Mongolian features sat cross-legged on a dais surrounded by a large entourage sitting on the floor. So absorbed was I that I didn't notice Ben arranging objects behind me with the attendant. I was surprised to see him enter beside me holding a tray of fruit, some gold coins among other items, all draped with beautiful white silk ceremonial scarves, or *kataks*, over the offerings. He bowed low as the guru brightened with a big smile and leaped up to embrace Ben ardently, head to head.

Chökyi Nyima Rinpoche, abbot of this Ka-Nying Shedrub Ling Monastery, was recognized as the seventh incarnation of a great lama, Gar Drubchen, an "emanation" of the second-century Indian master Nagarjuna, who was one of the most important philosophers of Buddhism. This illustrious teacher draped a *katak* around Ben's neck, put his hand on his own heart, patted it, and said, "Ben, my heart is so happy to see you."

For a moment they seemed to speak to each other with the intimacy of brothers. Tibetan Buddhists honor their root guru as their original main teacher in an intense way, but I had never witnessed an expression of this until now. My chest seemed to stiffen when I understood that this was my son giving this man so much honor and needing to return to him to report the progress he had made in his three-year retreat. Ben introduced me to the guru, and the guru embraced me (also head to head) and put a *katak* around my neck. He asked about my trip, how I was, and whether there was anything that I needed. Then he turned to Ben to discuss the content and quality of his recent retreat. As I watched this close friendship continue, the Rinpoche's entourage listened in respectful silence.

After their discussion, I presented him with my gift of the *Tanya,* and explained some of its terminology as I had done for Thây. A handsome Nepalese man about my age turned to me and, after asking my age and telling me his, said, "Maybe you will teach me and him," pointing to the man seated beside him. "He is seventy-two and quite a scholar." Indeed the elder man had taken the book and was examining it and asking me about it and its contents. I sat open-mouthed and wondered if this was the Nepalese version of a pass.

One of the women sitting at the Rinpoche's feet was someone I had met in the Thamel shopping area of Kathmandu; she took me aside and asked how I knew Ben and how Ben knew the guru.

"He seems to really love your son," she commented with awe. This became even more apparent after the entourage departed to leave the three of us alone. The attendant gave me a chair as Ben sat at his feet. These two friends continued a conversation that must have begun years ago; even though they hadn't seen each other in three years, it seemed that they hadn't missed a beat. For some reason, tears fell out of my eyes.

"How could you do that to me?" I asked, referring to the guru's sending my son away for three years. The Rinpoche laughed good-naturedly at my seeming jest. I laughed too, but even more tears slipped silently out of my eyes. I was very far from joking. Something in this intimacy drew audible sobs from me in spite of my attempt to suppress them. I had dreamed of such a relationship occurring between my son and the great rabbis of our time.

"You must take care of your mother," Chökyi Nyima said to Ben somberly, held his hands, and looked in his eyes; he was understanding our dilemma.

"I know," said Ben. "That is why I am asking you to arrange a transmission with your father for her peace of mind." The guru quickly agreed. I had no idea what they were talking about.

I yearned for the quiet and transformative mindfulness of Plum Village again. However, as Ben planned Plum Village as the first step in my gradual mind-change, so he must have reasoned out the steps of my transformation. He planned to open the door to an even deeper experience.

12

Pointed Teachings for an Old Woman

THE PEACE THAT I HAD TOUCHED IN PLUM VILLAGE seemed as scrambled as my morning breakfasts. Where in France I felt safe among vegetarians to maintain my kosher food observances, here I had to also make sure restaurant vegetables were washed and properly disinfected, eat only fruit with skins, and hope for some of Ben's kind American friends to invite us to their homes and honor his mother with safe vegetarian food. In addition, I had to be careful to avoid meat, since Tibetans, though they are Buddhists, are not vegetarians, owing mainly to the food availability, climate, and customs of their homeland. Jewish peddlers of the last century, who wandered from place to place, were known as egg-eaters because that food was kosher and thus a safe choice during their travels. Now, in my wandering, I had become like them, but what was I peddling? I had to be careful with my wares; the only customer who interested me was Ben.

Meanwhile, my serendipitous, easily distracted mind was constantly fractured by all the stimulation; this was a far cry from my tending the beloved greenhouse, a field away from plum orchards, grape vineyards, and the silent opening of flower seeds in the elegant French countryside. Even more critical to my adaptation was that I felt as if I had traveled backward in time after my stay at the Vietnamese hermitage. Buddhism as interpreted by Thich Nath Hanh seemed to be a blend of the Asian tradition with Western sensibilities. Thây was eclectic with his updated language, including references to G-d and Western religious traditions, and his creative, poetic version of "engaged Buddhism" applied to politics, ecology, and interpersonal relations. Of course the Dalai Lama is famous for his "free Tibet" campaign, taken up by many celebrities. Both varieties of Buddhism—the late-Mahayana Vietnamese, which was revived in Vietnam in the 1920s after a long period in which Confucianism dominated, and the Tibetan, which had a longer, uninterrupted historic stream—clashed with dictatorial regimes in the 1960s. Both varieties are also examining ways to integrate Buddhism with the West.

Here in Nepal, although it was a developing country with uncontrolled pollution, a juxtaposition of manual and mechanical methodologies, and an exotic mix of adventurers and natives, I had the feeling of being closer to the birthplace of the Buddha and the ancient origins of the Dharma. I had the sense of actually going back in time to the source of Buddhism—an intriguing thought, considering that my most recently acquired name was Going-through-Obstacles-to-the-Source.

The Tibetan Buddhism practiced here had been isolated from the outside world, perhaps because the Himalayas had physically, until this century, protected its heritage. The Tibetans had developed their transmission of Buddhism from its earliest introduction without interruption, and after the Chinese invasion of Tibet, Nepal received a large influx of fleeing Tibetan Buddhist refugees.

Buddhism was brought to Tibet by a sage of India, Padmasambhava, who had been invited to Tibet by King Trisong Deutsen in the eighth century. Four Tibetan schools developed in the following historical order: Nyingma, Kagyü, Sakya, and

Gelug. The Dalai Lama, although he is considered the spiritual leader of all Tibetans, belongs to the Gelug lineage, the most recent school, which began in the fourteenth century; Chökyi Nyima Rinpoche, is a unique blend of the Nyingma (the "Ancient School") and Kagyu lineages. According to Ben, each lineage has its own distinct character and emphasis.

Building on the earlier form of Mahayana ("Great Vehicle") Buddhism, Tibetan Buddhism is known as Vajrayana ("Diamond Vehicle"). Since its scriptural basis is the tantras, it is sometimes also called Tantric Buddhism, which teaches that one can attain Buddhahood in this very life. Contrasted with the stark simplicity of Zen, Vajrayana Buddhism appeared rich in mystical rituals, secret teachings, and elaborate iconography, with many deities; special emphasis seemed to be given to goddesses.

Tibetans believe strongly in the presence of living Buddhas, people who have attained complete enlightenment, and perhaps this makes it easier to accept that the individual practitioner can actually attain the Buddha-mind. Chökyi Nyima's father, Tulku Urgyen Rinpoche, was apparently one who had attained this awakened state, which Robert Thurman has described, in his *Essential Tibetan Buddhism*, as being "what theists have thought the mind of G-d would have to be like." Chökyi Nyima had told Ben that his father—who was his own root guru—was closer to the source than anyone else because he was born in Tibet and only recently made his way to Nepal, whereas his son had lived and practiced almost all his adult life in Nepal. I knew that Tulku Urgyen had undergone considerable training in mountain hermitages and spent many years in retreats, but I simply thought of him as being like a gentle biblical prophet living in a cave. I did not realize at the time how highly revered he was as a meditation master and a "realized being." Yet I did appreciate that meeting with Tulku Urgyen would be a rare and unusual event.

Physically, mentally, and spiritually, my awareness became glazed in a time warp when Ben immediately made arrangements for us to travel to Nagi Gompa monastery in the hills above Kathmandu to see Tulku Urgyen. Of course, third world time is even worse than Jewish time, which is always later. Here we traveled not knowing whether the wise man would even be there and, if he was there, whether he would be available. Perhaps, like disciples who used to wait in the vestibule for an audience with the Lubavitcher Rebbe in Brooklyn, we could wait for a long, long time. We could come back daily and still not know more about his availability than the day before. Besides, Ben was told that Tulku Urgyen was bedridden and suffering from health problems.

During the taxi ride through the countryside and up the curving mountain road, Ben gave me my instructions about Tulku Urgyen's health and the uncertainty of seeing him. The smog of Kathmandu disappeared in a bright horizon that made me queasy. We were driving toward the timberline when we came to an army watchpost. The monastery was on government land that required a fee to enter. I had heard that the topsoil in this country was endangered because of deforestation. During other mountain-hugging drives, I would see many trees whose bottom branches had all been cut for fuel, leaving their skinny trunks perilously waving in the wind. They looked like the puffed foliage of the trees in Dr. Seuss's children's books. The road clung to the mountainside as we rode the dangerous spiral higher and higher.

Finally the taxi left us at the bottom of an upward path with a summit hidden in the trees. The rest of the way was to be scaled on foot. I tried not to look down as I began the hike to the monastery. The angle was so acute that I hugged the side of the mountain as I huffed and puffed up. From every vantagepoint, it was a sheer direct drop to the bottom. I thought of Ben's friend Jane walking with her crutches up mountains like these on pilgrimage, and I kept repeating like a mantra, "If Jane can do it, I must do it." Ben ran ahead as I was passed by young, thin boys balancing lumber and bricks for the continual construction at the monastery, and then a team of German hikers whom I recognized from the Hotel Shakti.

One very vigorous woman about my age briefly took me by the hand and demonstrated a stout marching technique. "Like dis, and dis," she kept saying while she swung my arm high with each hike until her party was out of sight. She dropped my arm and ran ahead.

Ben expressed his hope that Tulku Urgyen Rinpoche would see me. Finally, after climbing the stairs to the top of the monastery, we were told that we would be received. We were escorted into a small room where an elderly man in maroon robes and a wool hat leaned against a pillow in an elevated bed. Facing his many Buddha statues, he was fingering his brown rosary beads and chanting in a low voice to himself. Bowing down, Ben presented him with gifts, orange juice, and fruit, all draped with fine kataks. I followed into the room but remained upright. He draped a silk scarf around each neck, like a Tibetan version of the Jewish prayer shawl, or *tallis*. Then the interpreter made the request for the interview.

"Yes, the Rinpoche will speak to you," said the interpreter as Tulku Urgyen assumed the lotus position on his pallet and began to speak. For the next hour and a half he instructed me on the nature of "mind"; as I listened, I thought that although he used the word *mind*, he was talking about G-d, and the ideas seemed to agree with some intuitive primordial sense of mine about the nature of the universe. A calm enveloped us during this "transmission," a special imparting of direct oral teachings. I remember his hands rising and falling, sometimes touching a cup or his beads to demonstrate a worldly example, sometimes meditating to demonstrate a mystical moment, and sometimes snapping his fingers to dispel the illusionary duality. There was a pace, a poetry to his timing, and a timelessness to the moment.

Finally, he asked me, "So, Ben's mother, now look inside. What do you see?" After a moment I told him what I saw; it was a luminously turning and arising movement that seemed self-perpetuating. It had no color but was the same clarity of a clear mirror without any reflection in it. It just kept rising and turning on itself. I could look at this forever and it brought me a peace that was beyond denomination. Was this an embodiment of one of the names of G-d? When I asked myself this, I noticed a large eye in my inner vision, the larger-than-life eye of my Plum Village dream.

I swear I heard him say, "Lahhh sooooo," with such an Asian rise of inflection that I was transported back to all the Charlie Chan detective movies of the forties and the fifties. He spoke again in that same rise-and-fall intonation with his hands orchestrating his instruction.

The interpreter, Erik Schmidt, a fair Danish man with an understated manner, said, "The Rinpoche does feel that Ben's mother sees. Now the Rinpoche would like her to look again. He says, 'So, Ben's mother, now look inside. What do you see?' He wants to know what it feels like."

Rinpoche smiled sweetly and looked at me very deeply.

After a long silence, I said, "It feels like home."

We shared another lovely silence.

As part of his teaching style of "personal experience," Rinpoche asked if I had any questions. At this point, I had no way of accessing anything like conceptual thinking. Ben, reading my state of consciousness, asked for instruction about my present approach to meditation.

"My mother," he began in his Tibetan English, "she makes meditation with the breath as support. So how should she incorporate this?"

"Lahh soo," replied Rinpoche, pacing his answer with his breath; "this is the ABC's of meditation." Tibetan meditation is full of elaborate visualizations, and Dzogchen, the Nyingma tradition of "great perfection," offers a long curriculum of mind-training to realize the consciousness of continual awakening. "This is called the original Buddha-mind," Tulku Urgyen continued, "which is empty. The reason why we can go to heavenly realms to be enlightened is because our true nature is empty cognizance. That which propels us is our own thinking." Knowing that this would take me years to digest, I shifted to ask a question about my Jewish practice.

"Rinpoche," I finally began, "in my tradition, for the past four years, I have been keeping the Sabbath faithfully from sunset Friday evening to sunset Saturday. I try not to disturb any electrical or motor energy, and do the prayers and readings. Just before sunset, if I do it correctly, something shifts in my consciousness. What is that?"

"The important thing is unoccupied mind, the unbusy mind. Not to do anything at all with the mind. The training here is just to leave the mind not doing."

I tried to not do, but conceptual thinking came back into play. Besides, the lesson was over. Would I be able to carry it with me down the mountain?

Tulku Urgyen was quite social after his instruction. He asked if we would like some tea, and we asked about his health. He lifted his garment up to show us a scar from his gallbladder operation, and he invited me to touch it. His skin felt silky-smooth like a new infant's. I was glad that we had brought him some juice, and I felt so tender toward this grandfatherly man, who had received me on his sickbed to alleviate my distress by teaching me to touch that endless peace.

Bowing and backing out when the Rinpoche seemed weary, Ben took me to the "Jewish Quarter" of the monastery, so named because most of the devotees there were Jews. During the evening *puja*, I went to a back room to jot down some notes for a column, called "From the Back of the Shul," that I write for a Jewish publication. Erik Schmidt had told me that what I had received were "secret teachings," only transmitted orally (perhaps, I thought, as the oral Torah once was). I was asked not to record the details of the transmission. So I put down my pen and tried to integrate an experience that is beyond words, beyond thought, beyond denomination, but somehow points me back to the mystical experience of the Jewish Ayn Sof, the One without End.

Days later, while visiting one of the caves that is a sacred Buddhist site, I told some other Western visitors that I had received a transmission; they seem surprised that I had been given so much time with Tulku Urgyen Rinpoche, as they had been sent away with merely a blessing. Subsequently Ben would clarify or explain more philosophical points to me. As time passed, those moments became more precious in my memory, for as it would turn out, Tulku Urgyen had barely a year to live.

While in the cave, to my surprise and delight I saw a stone carving of a Star of David. Later I learned that these interlocking triangles forming a six-pointed star are a Vajrayana Buddhist symbol.

Later that week, Chökyi Nyima received me and Ben in private again in the large golden shrine room. A writer and disciple had just left after presenting the Rinpoche with his book on the history of Tibet in Tibetan. (So other people gave books to gurus, not just me!) I learned that the transmission I had received from Tulku Urgyen was called "pointed teachings for an old woman." I realized that I had received a crash course in essential Buddhism. Again I was instructed not to write the details in any publication. The reasoning was not only that readers would not understand the bald words without the experience, but also that I would dissipate the blessings that I had received. The teachings must be carefully passed on to understanding and willing students.

Now I had the opportunity to ask Rinpoche about the necessity of bowing down to the Buddha and to teachers. Amused at my question, he said that this was merely a custom, and offered a rather unexpected example. Raising his right hand, he said, "In Asia we use our right hand for all our important functions. Whereas the left"—he raised his left hand and chuckled—"is used for bodily functions. Therefore I would never shake hands with you using my left hand!"

After I regained my composure, Chökyi Nyima began to instruct me in meditative visualizations involving light and rainbow colors, with the image of Shakyamuni Buddha as the focus. Because of his father's transmission, he assumed that this was the next step for me. However, I balked. "Couldn't I use the biblical matriarchs, like Miriam, instead of the Buddha? The Buddha is too foreign to me."

Chökyi Nyima turned to Ben and asked, "Who is Miriam?"

"A Hebrew saint," answered Ben.

"No problem."

Later I learned that what I had called idols were not actual deities being worshiped, but were images used in Buddhist meditation as focal points to develop worthy aspects of "Buddha-mind" in oneself.

I pressed him further and said that I felt the instructions that I received from his father on the nature of mind described the qualities of Ayn Sof, one of the Hebrew names of G-d. "The no-god of Buddhism," I said, "seems like the Ayn Sof, the without-end nature of G-d."

Again Ben translated, and again Rinpoche said, "No problem."

After more questions and answers, he blessed me and gave me the Tibetan name Shenpen Zongmo, which translates as "Compassion of the Source." Again I didn't bow down to him, and he understood.

13

Year of the Wood Boar: A New Beginning

LUCKILY, I CARRIED THE STILLNESS FROM TULKU URYGEN'S transmission throughout my Nepalese visit. In his foreword to Tulku Urygen's book, *Repeating the Words of the Buddha,* Chökyi Nyima describes his father's style, "instruction through personal experience," as a simple approach that is "saturated with direct, pithy instructions" that impart "the very heart of the awakened state. . . nakedly and directly." Afterward, however, this "glimpse of insight" can be continued only through the practitioner's efforts to "sustain the continuity." I resolved to find the stability and concentration from an ongoing practice suited to me. At the same time, I kept thinking that surely this naked state is common to all spiritual pursuits, before a particular system of language and heritage is superimposed. This thought was to become increasingly persistent in times to come.

After the indescribable calm of my moment on the mountain-top, my night's sleep became dreamless, with no more troublesome visions of golden calves or fearful electrifying energy. Thankfully, through the cacophonous noise and odors of Kathmandu, I had become like the bodiless eye of my meditation lesson with Tulku Urgyen and my Plum Village dream. Even in the midst of activity, I seemed to have a continuous, intuitive awareness of the interdependence of all phenomena that Tulku Urgyen had demonstrated, which the eye (my mind's eye?) was passively observing without emotion. I was happy to be in this state for the coming two-day Losar festival, the Tibetan New Year, celebrated on the new moon or "no-moon." It would include feasting, dancing, family visits, and parades for Nepalis and visitors alike.

Each Tibetan year took its name from one of twelve animals and one of five elements. This Losar was the Year of the Wood Boar. A boar year is said to bring the possibility of prosperity or waste, abundance or excessive indulgence. Wood is a symbol of vitality, growth, and awakening.

I saw examples of these themes during our activities and outings of the next few days. Everywhere we went, preparations were underway for the big holiday. The small street stupas outside the walled driveway to our Hotel Shakti were also being painted, so that its dwarf lions got redder and redder and their necklaces more and more golden each day that we walked by. Small shops were sprucing up their wares of handicrafts and garments. Private homes, hotels, and small rooming houses were getting ready for the tourists and pilgrims who would soon flock to the *gompa* (monastery) for prayers, lama-dancing, and festivities.

We journeyed west to the ancient Buddhist site of learning, Swayambhunath, whose terrace-summit held many *chaityas* (community meditation halls), small stupas, temples, and a *gompa* with its great stupa newly brightened for the new year. Ben and I climbed the three hundred stairs and passed all the stone sculptures and freshly painted statues of Buddha. At the top, the blue, yellow, and red painted eyes, always awake above a wise, OM-shaped nose, peered from all four sides of the summit. Just as in Boudhanath, numerous colored prayer flags fluttered from their ropes, releasing holy prayers, as pilgrims circled the stupa clockwise, turning the prayer wheels; irreverent resident monkeys leaped onto the giant statues guarding the four directions. The monk who lived in the monastery there lit up at the sight of Ben, claiming he remembered him from previous visits, and invited us to his room for a splendid view of the valley. Later, as we visited a shrine at the bottom, a local artist high on the wall surrounding the base continued to paint a deity golden. I snapped a picture of a slender young girl carrying twigs on her head as she posed by the prayer wheels for me; she seized the opportunity to beg a fee for modeling. Festivals are a vital time for beggars as well.

We welcomed the opportunity to escape the Kathmandu smog when Ben's friend K.P. took us to Dhulikhel, an hour's clear and sunny scenic drive east, to a resort with a panoramic view for dinner. We drove by a site that has drawn pilgrims for centuries, called Namo Buddha ("Hail to the Buddha"). Here the Buddha in one of his earlier incarnations was said to have been so moved with compassion for a mother tiger who was weakened and immobilized by hunger that he offered his own flesh as food for her so she could nurse the new brood.

The closer we got to the new year's holiday, the more I became aware that something was on Ben's mind. He kept telling me that we were scheduled to visit all his friends with their families, and all his Buddhist-devotee friends, including many monastery residents. With these social necessities approaching, Ben wanted me to dress appropriately to meet the important people of his Nepalese life. Ever since the episode with the gaggle of petite brown-skinned graceful women in their colorful Punjabis and saris at the airport, Ben began mentioning how good every passing Punjabi suit looked. He was hinting that I needed a makeover. I was dusty, travel-worn, overweight, and slow in my double-layered-walking-pants-hiking-boot-and-turtleneck garb. Every slightly heavy woman in a Punjabi motivated the same comments from my son:

"Mom, you would really look good in a Punjabi."

"Mom, I think you should buy those and wear them always."

The Punjabi consists of a knee-length dress with side slits covering ankle-hugging matching pants; I thought its typical bright colors and one-of-a-kind hand-stitched and sometimes handprinted designs looked good on the dark-skinned women here but probably wouldn't on this sallow, oversized American lady who didn't court the sun for tanning pleasures.

Finally, after one of our many mountain excursions with K.P. to get out of the Kathmandu smog, Ben asked him to take me to the shops his wife patronizes. Soon afterward I found myself watching Ben's old friend ply his influence with a shopkeeper far from the tourist centers. K.P. was my son's age, but unlike my son he was married with three children, the sole support of his mother, the owner of a carpet factory, and the sponsor of his brother's wedding and new house. He reminded me of a slim young Omar Sharif. In these shops that only Nepalis frequent, the bargaining was entirely in his hands.

As the only Western woman in the shop, I walked and talked differently from anyone else in sight. I was taller and broader than any Nepalese woman, and everything I liked was too small. The graceful shopkeeper kept unfolding the piles of Punjabis and then ordering her assistant to take them back. I worried at the pile of garments on the dressing room floor, but a snap of her fingers had them collected and hung. Finally we found one, an amazing bright pink maroon, with small pearl beads hand-sewn on all the edges and a bright purple and gold design that graced the bodice, curving and diminishing down the front of the dress. I needed practice to throw the matching shawl around my shoulders with the ends flowing behind me. My son could dress me up, but could he take me anywhere?

I walked out and down the open porch between the shops while K.P. began the bargaining; the neighboring shopkeeper who had failed to come up with my size peeked out with a where-could-I-find-a-Western-size-like-that? look. Re-entering the original shop, I noticed a white one with maroon and gold patterns; this obviously was cheaper than the other, but throwing it onto the bargaining table made the conversation more interesting. In a wink, the deal was made, the two Punjabis were wrapped, and we left with Ben smiling and K.P. commenting that his petite wife buys nine at one time.

The next evening at the Losar visits, we passed celebrants dancing around the stupa. Since the dancing reminded me of slow horas at Jewish festivities, and since I was so dressed up in my new Punjabi, for one moment it didn't seem that different from attending a bar or bat mitzvah. Actually, we went to an elegant buffet dinner in the shrine room of Chökyi Nyima's monastery, where the Rinpoche was holding court from his throne. Patrick, a visiting professional photographer, noticed my Punjabi and looked closely at the beads. He had just come from the Smithsonian, where he had been photographing the inaugural gowns of the wives of the early American presidents.

"Those are hand-sewn pearl beads just like Dolly Madison's!" he exclaimed. Standing beside us, my son smiled broadly. Whew! He *could* dress me up and finally take me someplace, as long as I didn't question too many things in this culture where the etiquette was sometimes beyond me. I'm afraid my comments about how I had wanted Ben to come home from his retreat puzzled the *khenpos*, ordained lamas with the equivalent of a PH.D.

When news of my transmission got around, some of the Westerners seemed interested and struck up conversations with me. One mother of a Buddhist devotee confided how her mental illness had become a severe affliction until she came to Nepal and was cured by a khenpo who used Buddhist psychology. Another woman, an expatriate American lawyer who had moved to Kathmandu with her family and who worked as an educator, seemed pleased to meet me and exclaimed, "You're Ben's mother, the one who knows the Hebrew tantric practices of the Hebrew goddess Mayam!" Ben laughed out loud at this, and later quoted it as an example of why he doesn't trust the gossip of the courtyard. At least he understood the consequences of *lashon hara*, the evil tongue. He immediately told her the story of how, after balking at Chökyi Nyima's instruction in rainbow visualizations using

Shakyamuni Buddha, I asked if I could substitute Miriam instead. She chuckled, turned to me, and began to tell me her story of healing from a deep paranoia by another lama who made her sit, "even if you don't meditate," for thirty minutes three times a day. He became available regularly for discourses about calming the mind and transforming her illness.

Her story confirmed my feelings about the spiritual poverty of current therapeutic approaches. I told her about my search in the seventies for help in calming my fears and emotional distress—how I had tried the Yogananda retreat but only became further confused; there were no American meditation teachers like these lamas and khenpos available to me at that time. Besides, I was uncomfortable with the statues of the yogi and of Christ. *And* there was a lot of bowing and supplication to gurus at that retreat; I remember my upright posture as I asked for the wisdom of Rabbi Akiva in that crowded room of prostrating seekers. Furthermore, I had heard of Rabbi Nachman's healing cures and of moments of *yichidut* (spiritual interviews) with other rabbis who interceded and prescribed prayer, service, and ethical behavior to come out of such lapses. My discussion with the American lawyer and her references to a systematic mind-science aroused my interest and motivated me to attend a course in Buddhist psychology at the Barre Center for Buddhist Studies after I returned home to Massachusetts.

Earlier that day, visits to the families of Ben's friends had invigorated me, especially seeing their respect for elders. K.P. and the idol-maker both housed their mothers in their homes and integrated them into family activities with courtesy and affection. The wives and mothers of both K.P. and the idol-maker were gracious hosts to me and continually served me with lemon tea and rice and vegetables. The urge to feed one's guests seemed as powerful in this culture as mine. Each sip that I took was taken as a signal for an instant refill. They all kept my tea glass so full, it was impossible to drain it. All were dressed in their best clothes, and all had adequate room in their large houses for their parents. They all called me "Mama." Somehow, during these visits, my relationship with Ben had become more peaceful and less contentious, in my mind anyway.

Nepal-born Tashi, another long-time friend of Ben's, treated me with respect and affection as he helped me cross streets with speeding motorcycles and cars. He had become a monk and personal assistant to Tsok Nyi Rinpoche, another son of Tulku Urgyen's and abbot of his own monastery in Kathmandu. We visited Tashi's parents, siblings, and nephew, who all lived together, while Tashi of course lived in the monastery.

These parents of Ben's friends, dressed in their rare Tibetan jewels and finery, were about my age. Ben told me that when the Chinese invaded Tibet, these people bravely took their children in baskets straddling a donkey and trekked over the Himalayas carrying their valuables (which they now wore!) until they reached the safety of Nepal. Their courageous flight seemed similar to that of Jews struggling to get out of Europe during World War II before it was too late.

On the second day of this two-day festival, we returned again in early afternoon by rickshaw to the entrance of Boudhanath to view the elaborate meditative day-long dancing of the masked lamas. Ben told me that the dancing was only recently introduced, and I looked forward to viewing these rites of renewal as we walked again past the many stalls. Now there were many more people than the time of our first visits, more hawkers selling relics, jewelry, and small violins, and many more pilgrims with colored strings in their hands and on their wrists, signifying the blessings they had received from the lamas. The dome of the stupa had its new whitewash completed now and was adorned with fresh golden arcs made with saffron water. This renewal of the stupa for the holiday would bring blessings to the devotee who sponsored it. The workman had to be especially skillful and accurate as he threw the colored water with a precise movement of his arm—a gesture like the meditative Asian art of calligraphy writ large.

More and more pilgrims kept crowding the walkway around the white mound, whose symbolic architecture represented the four elements of fire, air, earth, and water. There were Nepalese in Western suit jackets and Westerners in Nepalese jackets; many people wore the traditional *chuba*. The banners of prayer flags streaming from the top of the stupa to the bottom of the stairs had multiplied. Hundreds, maybe thousands, of prayer flags tied together on long, streaming ropes floated in the air. Some flags waved close to the tops of our heads. The belief is that these prayer flags would benefit the whole world, all sentient beings.

Intermittently, drums and music announced a service, and a parade of lamas commenced; they wore maroon robes with bright gold moon-shaped hats that followed the curve of their scalp. The lead lamas had golden flowered shawls on their shoulders, and one was carrying a large fabric parosol with long ruffles. They circled the stupa with a photograph of the Dalai Lama placed on a throne. There was barely enough room to walk. This village was an enclave of twelve thousand Tibetans, the largest number outside of their native land, and it seemed as if they were all here today.

In the middle of the open area the pilgrims turned toward this parade to form their open-palmed hands into a *mudra*, or mystical hand gesture, for the mandala-offering to the Buddhas of the three times—past, present, and future. Ben said that the way they held their hands—with fingers intertwined to point to the sky—was indicative of Mount Meru and the four celestial continents; it was the most auspicious thing one could visualize as an offering. They seemed to be praying with this *mudra*, which represents their entire universe. Puffs of colored flour or *tsampa* were thrown into the air and hung momentarily like a cloud at eye level.

The eight painted eyes on the stupa looked out in all four compass directions as the crowds seemed to multiply under their gaze. These eyes on the largest stupa in Nepal seemed to me like an unblinking sentinel guarding the community with compassion and warning of the punishment for misdeeds and evil thoughts. Maybe, I fantasized, they held the Buddhist Ten Commandments in a single OM—just as, in a midrashic tale, the whole Torah was said to be contained in the silent Alef, the first letter of the

Hebrew alphabet. The monument is called Khast, meaning dewdrops, because when there was no water to mix the mortar, the builders would collect night dew in spread cloths. There is a lovely Jewish prayer for dew, to me a universal symbol of soothing.

Now the devotees continually engaged in the ritual circumambulation while chanting prayers and turning the prayer wheels. White stone elephants guarding the stupa wore necklaces of flowers. A golden throne under another canopy awaited a teacher to bless the crowd. The aromas from burning juniper incense and the lighting of butter lamps filled the air. Old women fingered their mantra beads.

We passed by a huge tent with the interwoven knot of eternity, an auspicipus symbol, sewn under its canopy billowing in the wind. Ben said that a traditional Tibetan opera was being performed. At the edge of the tent held up on poles were the spectators, so close to the performance that the sound system really wasn't needed. Although of course I couldn't understand a word, the opera's uniqueness guaranteed that a memory was in the making for me.

The lower monastery courtyard, which only yesterday was quite empty, was now crowded with people milling around some kind of straw tepee. Up the stone stairs to the upper courtyard, we saw Chökyi Nyima Rinpoche on the roof with a large entourage of lamas, khenpos, and other rinpoches seated under umbrellas with their Coca-Cola bottles parked on the walls. Many spectators had climbed out onto the numerous ledges. Chökyi Nyima waved to us down below.

Before climbing the stairs to greet him, we walked by the downstairs shrine room full of floating cylinder fabrics and papier-mâché fierce masks mounted for display with swords framing them, ready for use in the lama-dance. I believe I recognized the black mask of Kal Bhairav, a form of the god Shiva that Ben had pointed out earlier in Kathmandu's Durbhar Square. Bhairav represents a terrifying destroyer of corpses, signifying ignorance. The statue of the cruel Bhairav in Durbhar Square was reportedly once used as a kind of lie detector; he was believed to punish liars by causing them to bleed to death on the spot. He was an appropriate choice to wield the ritual sword that cuts through ignorance and obscurations.

A friend of Ben's named Graham—a Jewish Buddhist descended from Rashi and Maimonides—led us on a tour of the lama-dancing preparations, which he said were seven days in the making. While he was showing us the masks inside the main shrine room, Tibetan women kept entering and placing rupees around the masks. Graham's sister Sarah, a therapist visiting from California, said of the Tibetan new year that "today is like Rosh ha-Shanah, Yom Kippur, and Passover, when we start over again."

After we all walked up to the roof where Chökyi Nyima Rinpoche was sitting with his entourage under large striped sun umbrellas, his first greeting when he saw me taking notes was, "Ah, Mama, are you writing your feelings?"

While Ben was taking pictures of us and the lamas getting ready on this sunny clear day, I remembered a time past when Ben brought home photos of masked festival dancing; then I was frightened of how his interest in these exotic rituals would take him far away from a Torah-observant life. Now I was fascinated, knowing my faith was stronger today and beyond the threat of this kind of theater. The performing lamas began to take the masks from the altar and don their amazing costumes to wield their swords and mirrors. Some anthropologists considered this rite to be an adaptation of the pre-Buddhist shamanistic religion known as Bön. For me it also called to mind the beginnings of theater in England and the mystery and morality plays of the medieval church that I studied in graduate school.

These Buddhist rituals were designed to throw out the old year, to cut through the illusion of the self, and to tame the selfish ego. The lama-dancing represented ridding oneself of obstacles to the awakened state. The mirrors reflected the truth that the root of the problem is always in ourselves. The monks wore exotic heavy silk dresses with long, ample Chinese sleeves that brushed the grass as they danced; they had obviously rehearsed this many-parted presentation for long hours. Silk aprons adorned with ferocious dragons and wrathful gods topped off the heavy flowing tent of silk. Their lama platform shoes covering their feet with intense gold fabric made them even taller and more formidable. With ferocious black masks and prominent white teeth and red lips, these faces were trimmed with small skulls for hair. The movements began with slow, regular, highly exaggerated circular steps. Repetitive chanting accompanied the percussion of cymbals, growling short horns, and long twenty-foot horns. All the dancers move synchronously, with a one-footed hop, a circle of their sword and body, followed by a slow, repetitious dance to attack the demons in the mirrors. We, the silent audience, were held locked in this musical T'ai Chi building to a faster and faster steady pace. The lamas raised and waved their sleeves again and again to form a regatta of silent sails, a rhythmic visual pattern. In this inner court a slow dervish dance, an artistic walking and dancing and moving meditation, moved in a pattern similar to my vision during the transmission. The energy built, climaxed, and receded as the dancers moved back into the monastery for an intermission.

A hawk had circled for the duration of the presentation. Before leaving Boston, I'd had a vivid dream of a hawk settling on a branch outside my living room window. It seemed so real that I had to tell Ben the next morning. He said that hawks are protectors and that it was a good omen. (When a hawk actually did land on that selfsame branch near our birdfeeder almost at sunrise one day after I had returned home, I thought I was dreaming again!)

Young clowns somersaulted into the circle. Their antics served as an intermission. A tall clown taunted a smaller one, who became the comic victim. Ben described how the smaller clown was a young lad who had been abandoned in a shopping center and adopted by the monks, but he continually ran away, an example of talent pushing the limits of its guardians.

A bleat of the long horns, the prolonged clash of cymbals, and a patter on the drum announced the next part of the drama. The dancers entered slowly, wearing extremely tall pointed hats with wide felt brims, each sporting a small skull that looked real; their bare faces were covered with black dots. They formed a circle almost filling the courtyard outside the monastery. Their hats each bore a large peacock feather and long, flowing rainbow-colored silk streamers tucked inside the back of the dancer's belt so that the streamers brushed the thighs, adding to the height of the hat. The dance leader entered, commanded the center of the grassy courtyard, and commenced the repetitive dance of the goblets. Young monks with copper tea kettles served constant tea offerings—which Ben said they visualized as an ocean of nectar—to these protector-dancers, who held their goblets up to be filled. Eventually the lamas blessed the tea and threw it into the inner circle of the dance.

Chökyi Nyima, wearing a scholar's hat shaped like a maroon teardrop with long flaps over the ears to the shoulders, led his entourage around his courtyard, and then down the stairs to the lower outer courtyard with the straw tepee. The orchestra followed as young monks held the ends of the long horns. The dancers formed another circle in this larger lower couryard. I watched from the stairs, snapping numerous photographs. The dance of the flaming bow and arrow was performed here with more meditative circular hop-hop-hops. The leader waved his arrow like a wand toward his target—the straw tepee. Each arrow release followed an elaborate slow aiming ritual.

This entire performance had begun when the sun was directly above us; now it kissed the tips of young trees and made the shadows lengthen. Twilight hindered the marksmanship and made accuracy more difficult, but finally the tepee was ablaze. A whole gunpowder arsenal exploded as firecrackers repeated their surprises from this enormous pyre. All obstacles were transformed into smoke and obscurations reduced to a blackened stain in the courtyard green. The rinpoches joined their dancing brothers as the atonal rhythms crescendoed. Finally the dancers dropped their butterfly arms and walked back up the stairs to the shrine room for an elaborate *puja*. Kataks were draped about everyone as a form of blessing, while a young monk served tea to everyone who followed. We left so that Ben could circle the stupa to turn the prayer wheels at this auspicious time for removing obstacles.

Our hotel lobby echoed with the various dialects of travelers. One guest, mistaking me for a devotee, asked whether the pageants had inspired me. Because of the mandatory rationing of electricity, he didn't see me smile. The dancing that had filled the plaza around the stupa on the way back was now filling our neighboring courtyard. The partying was to go on all night.

During the next few days, other beginnings took place as well. A Hindu festival in honor of Shiva, the awesome Hindu god of beginnings and ends, also occurred this month. While we did not go to Pashupatinath, the ancient route of Hindu pilgrims and loinclothed yogis, we observed the religious syncretism of Nepal as followers of one religion took part in the others' festivals, and even adapted some of the rites of the other faith into their own. This mutual give and take certainly seemed preferable to the wars between religious groups that raged elsewhere. As part of the collective fun and carnival season, children strung ropes across our rickshaws' paths and gleefully demanded a toll in a Nepalese trick-or-treat atmosphere.

The noisy revelry made me crave the isolated landscape of clean air. To be renewed by the mountains that I would never climb, I took a plane tour of the Himalayas. Here, without the clamor of ritual and masquerade pageantry, I saw the naked, ragged, jagged edge of the roof of the world. I saw Everest below me. Like uncut diamonds, the chilly snowcaps renewed that inner stillness as my eyes swept the horizon. The mood of every snowy crevice and shadow carried different shades of awe and insight to me. Frederick Lenz, in *Surfing the Himalayas,* describes the energies of different physical locations on earth, saying that some places "intersect with dimensions of great clarity" and make it "easier to meditate, to study, to learn, . . . and to see into other worlds." I thought of the Tibetan teachers who had been isolated for so long, high in their mountaintop monasteries, of the biblical prophets meditating in their caves, and wondered what my own house in Massachusetts could teach me. I felt the clarity of this place deeply and wanted to hold it all the way home.

Ben's friend Tashi, somehow sensing this need to be closer to the higher mountain air, took us to the mountain village of Nagarkot, past the "Restaurant at the End of the Universe" (a real restaurant named after the one in Douglas Adams's comic novel of that name) to watch the sunrise over this mountain range; our lodging offered one of the best views of the Himalayas from the northeast ridge of the Kathmandu valley. Hugging the side of the building in the cold dawn light, I could see from Annapurna to Kangchenjunga, a mountain beyond Everest. With this overview as my climactic tourist memory, I knew it was time to go home, finally.

Later, Ben, packing his bag with characteristic speed, tried to help me pack. I can't make quick decisions like him, and I don't blame that on our age differences. At eight he used to enter a store knowing exactly what he wanted. When we shopped for his bar mitzvah suit when men's leisure suits were the rage of the early seventies, we no more than entered the store than he said, "That's it!" And it was it! (We have pictures to prove the fact.) He handled the checkout at the Shakti Hotel with the same speed and added pleasantries; he had already paid for cheaper lodging nearer to Boudhanath. I wanted to take pictures of the owner in front of his carved imitation of the famous peacock window in Bhaktapur that we saw during the women's conference day trip to the shrines. I wanted to linger in the dining room for one last glimpse of Nepalese television. The end of our time together here was nearly in sight, and I couldn't yet see the next new beginning.

We walked to the intersection where a cluster of rickshaws were lazing along the curb. When their drivers saw us fully loaded with baggage, they immediately surrounded us with promises of cheaper fares. Suddenly I was the hurrying one, glancing down the road for cabs. A cab stopped quickly and, oh yes, of course, the driver insisted, the fare was just right. Well, it was for a while. I saw Ben doing the S-shaped jiggle of his head and stop. Suddenly the fare rose because Ben needed to drop off luggage at his Boudhanath hostel; suddenly it was so far to drive and, of course, there was the wear and tear on driver and vehicle; and suddenly there were other excuses for more bargaining. Ben teased the driver back, and the bargaining persisted good-naturedly until the airport. I was saying goodbye to Kathmandu—and more.

We drove by the stalls and shops crowded with goods hanging inside the windows, outside the windows, above the windows. Men with boxes full of balm, wooden games, jewelry, and whispers of hashish in our ear—all quickly inhaled with the smog of Thamel—all these I would probably never to see again. I said farewell to New Road where the seamstress talked of wardrobing movie stars, to the upstairs tailor who made my son-in-law's silk-shirt birthday present, to the royal palace, to the long row of foreign offices, to the larger, more expensive hotels, and, of course, farewell to the dream of staying at the luxurious Yak and Yeti Hotel.

And farewell to these five weeks of daily conversations with my son about odds and ends and anxieties and people and politics and the Buddhist teachings of his gurus. The content was not as important as the process. Another memory floated by my consciousness: a soiled letter found on the ground near a Boston subway stop, written by some daughter to her mother, detailing all the small and large physical and emotional events of her week. I carried this letter for years; I never had that easy intimacy of daily details with my mother, and prayed that I would have it, one day, with a child of mine.

And now I realized that I had it. Finally. Long overdue. This trip for me was a journey for new insights into my son's identity. Hopefully, it would yield the fruit of a new beginning for mine as well.

Writing alone in my journal in the New Delhi airport, I checked my Jewish calendar and realized that this Losar also began the Hebrew month of Adar, the month of masks when we celebrate Purim in remembrance of Queen Esther's saving the Jews from destruction . . . Esther, whose name means "hidden," and Purim, whose theme is finding the holy, the *yod, heh, vav, heh* (the Hebrew letters signifying the mystical name of G-d) in the always renewable hidden places of our life.

14

Home for Shabbat

WITHOUT BEN TO TAKE CARE OF THE TRAVEL DETAILS, it was now my turn to pace the holding lounge in the New Delhi airport. I had extended my school vacation by arranging for substitute teachers in my absence, but now I needed to get back to work at the Hebrew school. Ben planned first to spend private time with Chökyi Nyima Rinpoche and then to go trekking with friends at Pokhara in the geographical center of Nepal.

I tried to make friends with all the women and children traveling alone so I could at least doze without anxiety of theft. I approached a beautiful young woman in army fatigues, one of the many Israelis who go mountain-climbing in Nepal after completing their army obligations; I asked her to watch my luggage while I used the ladies' room. During my only visit to Israel, I had seen many of these Amazons carrying their automatics, and I felt quite assured no one would dare go near my assortment of bags. In the ladies' lounge, when the attendants asked a dollar for each sheet of toilet paper, I felt obliged, in the face of their poverty, to pay and not bargain. Ben's frugal management left me with a good surplus of money for the trip home. When I told my new friend about my restroom donation, she laughed and unpacked a thirty-inch carved statue of a beautiful woman.

"How much do you think I paid for this beautiful wood carving?" she asked. I dared not guess; I could see her reducing the Arabs of the Jerusalem *shuk* to tears from her bargaining. Ironically, the statue was an idol of Tara, a Buddhist *yidam* or deity, who embodies the divine feminine aspect of compassion—I looked her up in the guide to Buddhist gods and goddesses that I had bought. Obviously, this Israeli was a secular Jew who had never entered a synagogue and was at home in the singalongs of her Tel Aviv cafés; no observant Jew would bring this back to Israel. With almost no coaxing, she told me that she paid the wood-carver a fraction of his asking price. On the basis of Ben's tutoring, I realized that the craftsman had suffered a financial loss to save face. Unwittingly, this young Sabra, typical of those who are polarized against the Orthodox Israelis, had purchased an idol, whose hand gestures symbolize the act of teaching, to rest on her mantelpiece at home. Tibetans had been doing this for centuries to enlist the deity as a household protector and teacher. Some Buddhists would believe that the sight of this idol alone could influence change in the viewer. And many Orthodox Jews would consider it a near-apostasy to bring an idol into one's home.

Weary from these thoughts plus the all-night stopover, I sighed and tried to doze on my soft luggage. I knew that the implications of her action and my realization were beyond translation. I had to gird my loins for the jet lags ahead through many time zones, as I would travel against the earth's turn to gain time. I had one more long stopover in Paris, where, thank goodness, the airport architects supplied weary travelers with chaise lounges for quick naps. There was to be another stopover in New York also, so I had plenty of time through fitful bouts of sleep and reverie to review my trip, which was so full of filial, spiritual, sociological, and anthropological associations.

My flight dreams consistently filled with the symbol of a carved Jewish star whose center was embedded with the Sanskrit sign for

OM, whose three sounds, A-U-M, form the mantra of Buddha, Dharma, and Sangha. During the trip, to ensure against travel damage, I had packed and unpacked from my carry-on luggage a wood carving of the Jewish star with an OM in its center, a gift for my husband. I wondered if I was dreaming or awake in some enlightened moment when I smelled the familiar aroma of caffeine: a flight attendant was serving me coffee. Finally I was awake enough to realize that Boston was not that far away, nor were the waiting ears of my therapist husband.

"Sandy!" I called out and raced through security to begin a nonstop sharing. Again I was impressed with the irony that it was I, the cynic, the skeptic, who eventually made this trip to Shangri-la, not the original true believer, my husband. If he felt any deprivation because his health and disposition prevented him from surviving the strain and struggle of time-zone hopping, he never voiced it. Instead he seemed happy to listen and laugh and vicariously enjoy the numerous events and insights. The story of my Jewish Buddhist friend's recovery from mental illness through the guidance of a lama reinforced his long-held professional view of the need for a spiritual psychotherapy to illumine the vast darkness that some of his patients endured.

I got to our dining room just in time to light the Shabbat evening candles. During the next day, we took long walks along the aqueduct clearings in our suburban town and considered ourselves rich, even though we were, like many grandparents we knew, house-rich and cash-poor. This was a time to remember how much we had survived and endured, and not dwell on our battle scars. This was also the time of what the rabbis call Shabbat Zakhor, the Sabbath of Remembrance before Purim, commemorating the escape of the Jews of Persia from extinction through the intervention of the Jewish queen, Esther, and her cousin, Mordechai. There are always extra Bible readings for each Jewish holiday to bring out the meaning of the occasion. The Torah portion for this Shabbat concerns Amalek, one of the greatest villains of Jewish history, who led an attack against the Israelites during their flight from Egypt, preying upon the weak who had straggled behind the rest of the tribe (Exodus 17:8-16). Haman, the evil prime minister who plotted against the Jews in the Esther story, is said to have been a descendant of Amalek, as was Hitler. The reading reminds us to be mindful of the hidden Amalek in larger political or more intimate interpersonal realms.

The regular Torah portion for that Shabbat, *Vayikra* (Leviticus 1-5:26), enumerates various levels of atonement for sins and the appropriate sacrifices. In ancient times, when Jews worshiped at the Holy Temple in Jerusalem, atonement was accomplished through various sacrificial offerings of animals or grain; after the destruction of the Temple, when these sacrifices were no longer permitted, prayer services became the substitute, and the rabbis considered it a higher form of worship. In the companion Haftorah reading from the Prophets (Isaiah 43), the Jewish Babylonian exiles are warned not to take up the idols of other nations and not to forsake the One G-d.

Had I let any of these warnings go unheeded? During the Saturday afternoon rest and quiet, I questioned each experience. Intermittently I told Sandy about them, especially the "bow or not to bow" incidents. Surely I had not bowed to deities, demigods, or Buddha icons; but had I inadvertently brought a "hidden Amalek" back with me—not in the form of a goddess figurine like the one my Israeli acquaintance displayed, but in a more subtle, psychological or spiritual sense? Perhaps, by attending the various Buddhist rituals, I had not followed the letter of Jewish law; yet I could not discount the peace and awakening I had experienced. I felt that this was an authentic, primordial inner experience that transcended the differences between the religions.

As Amelek and apostasy can be hidden, so can the divine sparks. One of the mystical interpretations of Purim is based on the root of the name Esther, translated as "hidden." Significantly, the name of G-d is never mentioned in the whole Book of Esther, and the rabbinical sages drew from this fact the teaching that G-d is hidden. The *Zohar* teaches that although Purim and Yom Kippur are at polar opposites of the Jewish calendar, yet each is hidden in the other. On Yom Kippur we fast to empty ourselves for atonement; on Purim we feast and drink—and by tradition, one is to get so drunk that one can no longer tell the difference between Haman, the villain of the Purim story, and Mordechai, the hero. Thus duality is dissolved in the Ayn Sof.

Soon it was time to go back to work as a Jewish educator. While I had taught all age groups from young children in classrooms to the elderly in their apartment complexes, this time I was facing the galloping gonads of an impatient preteen group. This was the age, according to recent studies, at which children often decide to abandon their heritage. I remembered talking to an American Jewish Buddhist in Nepal about her childhood Jewish education, which she said was not inspiring. I had to admit that, while my grandson's day school does not fall into this category, supplementary Jewish education does run a poor competition with secular after-school activities like soccer. Here is where more doors have to be opened to the essential experience of the Divine. This difficulty was undoubtedly widespread in all religious education in our country today. If we don't interest our adolescent children in spirituality or idealism, they may be lost forever to secular materialism. I had to plan my strategy for telling my impressionable students about my trip so that it would sound interesting to them but not too exotic and tempting.

As soon as I entered the classsroom, the kids were unusually attentive. "Tell us all about it—please!" I tried to get them to appreciate the value of a different culture. I told them about some of the differences in the society and customs between America and Asia, about the widespread poverty in Asia, and the need that we all have for some spiritual dimension in our lives. I showed them the pictures I had taken of schoolchildren like them and also a photo of a girl with a bundle of thin fire twigs on her head, begging for rupees. I told them how some children their age were promised in marriage, sent out to work, and sometimes entered into religious life as monks or nuns. I hoped these American youngsters would appreciate how privileged they are in a material sense and perhaps gain a sense of thankfulness for their opportunities. It is ironic how materialism can exclude spiritualism, and how Buddhists and Hasidim alike often avoided wealth. Because of my immigrant family's escape from persecution and economic suffering in Poland, I felt lucky that Ben appreciated spiritual beauty in the midst of poverty and material suffering.

"Please wear your Punjabi," asked one girl whom I had been trying to help with her self-image because she kept calling herself slow. I couldn't refuse, especially during Purim, that festive time when Jews dress up in costumes. Israeli children in their costumes turn Israel's streets into a Jewish Mardi Gras. They carry baskets of sweets not for trick-or-treat mischief, but for gifts of food to be delivered to friends and relatives. Additionally, something is customarily given to the poor.

"Awesome." "Cool." These were the reactions at the next class when I appeared in my "Dolly Madison" bejeweled outfit. They certainly were paying attention. I decided to use this rare moment to introduce meditation. Immediately some of them held their hands up with thumb and forefinger touching, reminding me of a Buddhist *mudra*. They had definitely had some experience with this somewhere. I clarified that the exercise was to be in *Jewish* meditation.

"No such thing!" They had never heard of this variety.

"There are two thousand forms of meditation," I said, "and your hands only indicate one form. Jewish meditation has its own style." *Now* what was I to do? Suddenly I held my hands up in the gesture of the High Priest of the Holy Temple: each hand forming a V between paired fingers. This gesture is repeated as a part of holiday services where descendants of the priestly class, the Kohanim, bless the congregation.

"Anyone know what this means?" I asked. Suddenly I had a brainstorm and gave them a hint. "You've seen this on television!" No one remembered, perhaps because they were too young. "Doesn't anyone watch *Star Trek*?"

"The sign of the Vulcan high priest!" My brightest and most mischievous student got the right answer.

"You can now go on *Jeopardy*!" I said, referring to the popular TV quiz show. "Leonard Nimoy, the actor who played that part on *Star Trek*, is Jewish and knows this sign. He decided to incorporate it into his role." While this caught their attention, I led them in a brief meditation, slowly uttering the six words of the Shema, the watchword prayer of Judaism that declares our belief in One G-d, once taught to me by Rabbi Nehemia Polen after an exercise in Aryeh Kaplan's book *Jewish Meditation*. My elaboration and embellishment of this exercise began, after brief instructions in the meditative posture, by slowly focusing on the breath, listening to the silence between breaths, saying the Hebrew words slowly, visualizing light, bringing prayers for things money can't buy to the light, waiting for the silence between the breaths, and closing with a slow "amen" exercise. This was to become incorporated in every class I taught.

When I arrived home from teaching, I read a notice in the Boston *Jewish Advocate* announcing a workshop on Jewish mysticism given by a Lubavitcher Hasidic rabbi from abroad; I had to attend. I needed an answer to the dilemma created by the fact that my Buddhist experience seemed to confirm the Ayn Sof, while conventional Judaism denied Buddhist theology.

The following Sunday, I arrived in a spacious home overlooking the North Shore's view of the ocean. Soon the rabbi was outlining some points about the *Tanya* and answering questions about Abraham Abulafia, the thirteenth-century Sefardic mystic who meditated on the Hebrew letters. There is an entire mystical method of interpreting texts, called Gematria, involving the Hebrew alphabet, including the numerical values attached to the letters.

Some sages relate the letters to the *sefirot*, or steps of the ladder to Jewish enlightenment. Each step has an attribute, such as Binah (understanding), Gevurah (strength or justice), and so on. Soon we were deep in a meditation climbing the ladder and transforming ourselves into Alef, the silent first letter of the Hebrew alphabet. I had never been led through such an exercise before, only read about it.

After the workshop, I briefly told the rabbi about my trip and how I had given a copy of the *Tanya* to each teacher. ("I'm so proud of you," he said.) I told him about my son the Buddhist, and recalled how an Israeli rabbi told me that "he could lose his soul in Buddhism." I asked the rabbi whether we have Jewish souls, and whether a Jewish soul could become Buddhist.

"Our Jewish souls always remain Jewish and true to their nature." I felt vastly relieved and later found continued consolation in Frederick Lenz's *Surfing the Himalayas*, where he described how our innate nature has a certain frequency and tends to be attracted to compatible groups with similar or resonating frequencies.

I wrote to Jonathan Omer-Man, who runs Merkatz in California, an organization dedicated to Jewish mysticism. I was in pursuit of a curriculum that I could follow. The Tibetan system had developed its own series of gradual techniques toward its goal of awakening, but I wanted one true to my own tradition.

Next, I joined a meditation group in a local synagogue and was also involved in a satisfying study group with an Orthodox rabbi who had a PH.D. in Jewish mysticism. However, I wondered, if there is a Jewish path to enlightenment, where were its teachers? While the oral teachings of the Tibetan tradition had been preserved in an unbroken chain through its lineage of teachers, their original presence was no longer available. With the Tibetans in exile from their homeland and their culture being destroyed, the last of the old masters born in Tibet are aging. Similarly, in Jewish history, the Holocaust is the most recent comparable interruption in the unbroken mystical lineage from Sinai. The Shoah has also taken its toll on the masters of the Jewish tradition. Like the Jews, Tibetan Buddhists will have to receive the teachings from descendants of the great teachers or from written sources.

During the ensuing year, I realized that I had to return to Israel. Somewhere in the length and breadth of that country, I hoped to find my own evidence for the prolonged study and practice of a genuine Jewish mysticism.

15

Of Poetry and Palestine

WHEN I WAS ELEVEN I HAD CHOSEN MY DENTIST BECAUSE he was a published poet. One day, while I was seated in his dental chair, after he finished his prodding and picking, he asked me to recite a poem that I had written. Delighted to remember the day that inspired me—the day on that crowded Detroit high school field celebrating the birth of the state of Israel, amazed that every one around me was a Jew, determined to learn the conversational Hebrew that rang in my ears, and dreaming of becoming a pio- neer on a kibbutz—I told him my first poem:

> As birds come home to roost again,
> As people come to dine,
> So came the Jews from all the world,
> To live in Palestine.

I may have had cotton in my open mouth, so I'm not sure how well he heard me, but he gave me a kindly smile. Of course, Jews don't refer to Israel as Palestine anymore, because that name has been retained by our Arab cousins and is loaded with an embattled history.

To this day all things Hebrew inspire me to write poetry, and I am grateful to contribute my liturgical poems to Jewish prayerbooks and anthologies. I was happy for a time to serve as *gabbai*, the facilitator of Sabbath Torah readings for bat and bar mitzvahs, because, when I heard a young voice chant Torah, it reminded me of that pubescent moment when I fell in love with Israel. Only during my younger daughter's residency there did I finally get to visit, in February 1993.

As my tour guide choosing the important sites to visit, Rebecca took me to the tombs of our patriarchs, matriarchs, and sages. For that spiritual-poetic pilgrimage, I needed to go to Safed, once the rival of Jerusalem for its scholarship, where the saints of Jewish mysticism lived, wrote, practiced, and prayed; they concentrated here in flight from the Spanish Inquisition. Perhaps this place, one of the highest in Israel, was a Jewish Shangri-la, as Perle Epstein had suggested in her book *Kabbalah*. It was the birthplace of Jewish mysticism. Here the disciples of Abraham Abulafia could be found meditating on the different states of consciousness embodied in each letter of the Hebrew *alef-bet*, exemplifying the methodology known as permutation of letters, culminating in pronouncing various names of G-d. Here the legendary Isaac Luria, the Kabbalist known as the Ari (the Lion), taught his numerous disciples about the ten *sefirot*, the rungs of the ladder culminating in enlightenment. It was here that the white-robed mystics danced toward the edge of the forest, singing mystical hymns, to greet the Shekhinah, the feminine Divine Presence, as the Sabbath began at sundown. And it is here that over a hundred thousand pilgrims come in May to begin to celebrate the anniversary of death of Shimon bar Yochai, the attested second-century author of the Zohar, who hid from Roman persecution in a cave for thirteen years, meditating on the mystical meanings of Torah.

Then I had to go to the grave of the kabbalistic poet Shlomo Alkabetz, who wrote the mystical love poem "Lecha Dodi" (Come, My Friend), welcoming the Sabbath Bride, which is now a permanent part of the Sabbath liturgy. My daughter reminded me that it was forbidden to pray directly to these Jewish saints, for that would be an act of idolatry. Jews only pray to the Holy One "on the merit of" the departed saint. So I prayed that I should write well on the merit of Shlomo Alkabetz, that my poems be brought down from the Holy One of Words.

"Give me the words," I asked, as I do almost every time I write, "that I may write to glorify You. Give me the wisdom to choose the right words. And give me words of wisdom to glorify the Truth of Your Word. Grant me this on the merit of your sage Shlomo Alkabetz." On that cloudy day facing the wadi in front of the rolling hills of northern Israel, over the freshly painted blue tombstones, in full view of the trees, I listened for an answer. The trees have more than leaves on them, for rustling in the wind are long papers of prayers and supplications hung by pilgrims. I asked for this then and I continue to ask for this, as long as I am a writer.

Before leaving the cemetery, pilgrims often make one last heart-felt request at the mound of stones that is the grave of the talmu-dic sage Pinchas ben Yair. It is customary to circle his grave seven times, praying for one's need or desired trait. According to legend, Pinchas implored his students not to build a monument at his grave. They disobeyed, and at the end of the seven days of mourn-ing it collapsed; no one dared to disturb the disarray of stones.

This trip occurred the year before my visit to Nepal, but now I had to return to Israel to recapture that inner feeling of home that I found on the Himalayan mountaintop and the peace that I felt at the French hermitage. While in Israel, I would attend the Con-ference for Alternatives in Jewish Education (CAJE), an annual week-long meeting at Hebrew University on Mount Scopus in Jerusalem.

Since my Buddhist son had orchestrated new insights for me, I was searching for a new spiritual paradigm big enough to encom-pass these nondenominational experiences. In my dreams, the Safed pilgrims circling the sage's grave kept merging with the pil-grims circumambulating the stupa at Swambunath to turn the prayer wheels, and I would wake wondering what country I was in and what religion.

Upon my arrival in Israel, Rabbi Nachman of Breslov, the last great master of meditation and great-grandson of the Baal Shem Tov, was in my thoughts. He expressed the pull of the City of David, bred into the Jewish soul, when he wrote, "Wherever I go, I go to Jerusalem." The Passover seder concludes with the promise "Next year in Jerusalem!" At the conclusion of the wedding ceremony, the happy Jewish bridegroom breaks a glass underfoot in remembrance of the sad side to our tribal wheel of fortune—the destruction of the Holy Temple in Jerusalem; and the Jewish songwriter Jeff Klepper sings about "coming home to our future, to the place where we began." Many *olim*—Jewish immigrants who have fulfilled the dream of making *aliyah* ("ascent") to our ancestral homeland—kiss the ground at the airport upon disembarking from their plane. A custom also for first-time pilgrims, this prostration was enacted by many Holocaust survivors after the birthing time of the Jewish nation, by many refuseniks from the former Soviet Union after fleeing persecution, and by many black Ethiopian Jews flown to Israel in "Operation Moses."

Before heading for the university and my conference, I immediately went to the Western Wall, or *Kotel*, the last remnant of the Holy Temple compound, to search for that homely peace. (The term "Wailing Wall" is popularly used by foreigners but is considered irreverent by the pious.) Wending through the summer traffic of the Kotel Plaza, I found a place in front of the Wall in the middle of the women's section, opened my prayerbook, and tried to pray. The day's activities included entourages of many beautiful brides saying their last virginal prayers here; it is said that G-d especially heeds the prayers of a bride. The Shekhinah, the Divine Presence, never leaves the Wall, and *kvitels*, personal prayers written on folded pieces of paper, are inserted into every available crevice between the boulders. Some prayers were even tied, Buddhist fashion, to the shrubs that manage to cling to and canopy from the upright wall. Because of the crowds, I barely had room to approach one of the boulders to insert the *kvitels* given to me by friends at home.

When I came to the Amidah, the central Jewish prayer, recited silently while standing, I could barely concentrate amid the crowds of women and girls milling about and praying. Less distracted than I, scores of women beside me ran through their prayers like a meditation mantra, just like the Hasidim of old. "Open my lips," goes the opening prayer to the eighteen blessings of the Amidah, "that my mouth may declare Thy praise."

I was okay until the prayer for peace that includes these words: "Oh, grant peace, happiness, blessing, grace, kindness, and mercy to us and to all Israel. . . ." Then I lost it. There was no peace in Israel, not between the Jews and their Arab cousins nor among the various Jewish factions. Newspaper photos of the victims of war and street bombings came to mind. The assassination of Yitzhak Rabin was still fresh in my awareness, now in August 1996; my children had pleaded with me to be careful and not to ride buses. Two days after the signing of the peace treaty by Arafat and Rabin on the White House lawn, when my hope for my homeland was less fractured, I had written this prayer-poem:

PRAY FOR THE PEACE OF ISRAEL

"And Esau ran to meet him . . . and he kissed him . . . and they wept." —GENESIS 33:4

O Holy One of Peace, be with us now
In these scarred historic battlefields,
In the lingering remembrance of bitterness and loss,
And in the mined memory of war.

Forgive us for the hatred of our kin.

Let the children of Isaac and the children of Ishmael
Finally melt their swords to ploughshares.
Let Sarah and Hagar be equal so Abraham can smile again.
No more sibling rivals for this heart land,
Where we all return as prodigals from home.

Grant us wisdom to repair our grief with sweet sown seed,
So the long arm of time bring new-grown fruit,
Bright harvests, and lyric celebration;
Oh make us whole again with each season's round.

Bless these two brothers to touch more than hands;
Make them touch their hearts and souls
Until they see themselves, and You,
In one another's eyes.

As I thought of these words, my teary eyes could barely see the huge framed blocks with smooth, finished centers artistically hand-picked by some skilled mason, closely held in place by their own weight, set there by terrible King Herod. He rebuilt King Solomon's Temple after the Babylonian destruction and Jewish exile of 586 BCE (around the time of the birth of Buddha in Nepal), and wanted it to be the most beautiful building imaginable, as an act of vanity. Ruling from 37 to 4 BCE, he murdered Jewish leaders and scholars, and the Hasmonean wife whom he married to gain Jewish favor. I felt neither at home nor at peace remembering this.

The original boulders of Solomon the Wise, placed around 958 BCE in the inner sanctum itself for the Holy of Holies, the "dwelling place for the Lord"—these were all unavailable to me. Were they buried under my feet? I turned and went through the Dung Gate to circumambulate the outer wall of the Old City toward the Jaffa Gate; perhaps the whole face of my history would be more available in the outside stone walls surrounding the original city. I wanted these boulders to talk to me. With these stones as my witness, I practiced Thây's "deep looking."

I imagined King David, three thousand years ago, bringing the traveling, Divinely designed Ark of the Covenant housing the Ten Commandments to rest in the Tabernacle in old Salem, the city of peace, his new capital; he renamed it Jerusalem. He placed the Ark holding the Ten Commandments, that Jewish holiest of holy places, here. I imagined him dancing and singing—"Jerusalem is built like a city bound together, for there the tribes ascend" (Psalm

122). I imagined the Nazarites taking their ascetic vows, praying all day, and, even though I have no evidence of this, probably following some meditation practice during their period of abstinence.

I wanted to find Solomon's large hewn stones with rounded corners, with a smooth finish and dry construction, for the Holy Temple, Bet ha-Mikdash, or house of the sanctuary, a dwelling place for the Lord. He chose the site because it held the history of Abraham's willingness to offer his son as sacrifice. I imagined the high priest with his high hat, his long tunic and hem of golden bells, and his oracular breastplate; I saw him as he entered the Temple's inner chambers alone on Yom Kippur to utter the awesome name of G-d. He wore a rope around his waist as a precaution, in case the face-to-face experience with Divinity killed him; since no one else could enter the room with him, his body could then be pulled out by attendants holding the other end of the rope outside the room.

Then I remembered the Syrian conquest of Babylonia after Herod, their attempt to force Jews to worship their idols, and the Maccabean victory over King Antiochus' desecration of the Temple, celebrated at Hanukkah.

In the Roman war that followed, King Titus destroyed the Second Temple by fire in 70 BCE, leaving only that outer Herodian Wall; on the holiday of Tisha b'Av, Jews commemorate this destruction with the singing of the Book of Lamentations while seated on the floor of the synagogue, a posture of mourning.

With no locus for the Temple sacrifices, local worship began to be established in synagogues, and with the rise of Christianity, anti-Semitism flourished. I lapsed into disturbing memories of being chased as a child by neighboring children who accused me of the murder of Christ.

Wherever one goes in Jerusalem, every new building by law has Jerusalem stone for its exterior. The larger stones of the Byzantines (324–638 CE), the proselytizing Crusaders (1099–1187 CE), the Turks (1517–1917 CE), and this century's smaller 15-by-9-inch stones all carried to me the sadness of present and past battles.

While my mind was racing with these fevered meditations, I had arrived at the Jaffa Gate without realizing it, and remembered that I needed to get to Hebrew University before the onset of the Sabbath at sundown. I boarded a bus for a quick getaway. No such luck! The bomb patrol with its many police, ambulances, and cars had stopped traffic. Finally I hailed a cab to the CAJE site. Perhaps there I would find the impossible connection that I sought.

CAJE, the largest North American Jewish educators' membership organization, had been introduced to me at a critical period of my life shortly after my layoff from the corporate world when I was floundering for direction. In 1992 I was invited to read my poetry at one of their conferences, where I encountered amazing talent, diversity, and flexibility. CAJE embraces all approaches, from the Orthodox, Conservative, Reform, Reconstructionist, and Jewish Renewal, to unaffiliated and alternative. With two thousand delegates attending a choice of four hundred conventional and unconventional workshops in history, language, Halakhah, and the Bible as well as Kabbalah, meditation, and even a T'ai Chi interpretation of the Hebrew alphabet, and evening performances including storytelling, Jewish gospel, and rock versions of the Hebrew prayers, biblical events, and modern life, I had found inspiration then. I hoped for it again now.

The opening-night concert included well-known Israeli pop singers' tributes to the recently deceased Shlomo Carlbach, a modern Hasidic singing rabbi whose melodies or *niggunim* became a modern form of singing meditation. In past conferences, the songwriter Debbie Friedman had led the CAJE choir (with me in it) in her interpretation of Reb Nachman's prayer:

> You are the One, for this I pray,
> That I may have the strength to be alone.

Another reference to being alone is found in the Hebrew word for meditation, *hitbodedut*, whose root means, according to Rabbi Aryeh Kaplan, "mental self-seclusion." Perhaps Jewish meditation will flourish again through the efforts of Jewish educators such as these members of CAJE, who are known for "pushing the envelope."

Friday-night services presented a menu of all the available Jewish choices, and I prayed that the universal acceptance of all paths could be present in Israel. Overlooking an expansive view of the Judean hills from the Hecht synagogue on campus, I found moments of quiet prayer with a sisterhood of women in the silent Amidah. The Hasidim chant the service with a meditative tone, in a trancelike state, and I wanted this kind of experience in prayer too.

The Torah portion for the next morning was *Shoftim* (Deuteronomy 16:18–21:9), which includes Moses' song-poem of the Israelite history and the moral code that was given them. As I viewed Jerusalem from Mount Scopus that night, I thought about how Moses, before he was "gathered to his people" on Mount Nebo, was denied entry to the Promised Land—according to rabbinical commentary, because the anger he expressed in the desert was unseemly for a chosen leader. Even though Moses pleaded to be allowed to come back as a bird flying over these Judean hills, G-d said no. Here I was, overlooking the lights of the Holy City itself. How did I, no chosen leader, get so privileged? Even so, there was no burning bush for me here, no mountaintop vision.

The Haftorah reading from Isaiah gives comfort to the Babylonian exiles because G-d and Israel will be together again when they happily return to their beloved land. Isaiah channeled G-d's words to the Jewish people: "Wake up! Wake up! Don your strength, of Zion" (52:1). The commentary in the ArtScroll Chumash says, "Exile is most pain when there is no tomorrow, but not when we take to heart that G-d remembers us." I thought of the Dalai Lama and the Tibetans as exiles from their own land; I remembered how he called leading Jewish figures to Dharamsala (as reported in Rodger Kamenetz's *The Jew in the Lotus*) to understand how they have kept their religion alive in the Diaspora. These Torah and Haftorah readings lent more feeling to my return to Israel. They made me realize how I continually thought of

Buddhist memories in my Jewish surroundings and Jewish memories in my Buddhist surroundings. Yet no matter how hard I tried, I still could not come to any sense of resolution of my conflict between the two.

After the Shabbat meal, as part of the customary grace after meals, we sang Psalm 126, which alludes to the return to Zion after the harsh Babylonian exile:

> When the Lord brought the exiles back to Zion
> We were as in a dream.
> Then were our mouths filled with laughter
> And our tongues ringing with song.

Prime Minister Begin had chanted this psalm on the White House lawn after signing a peace treaty with Egyptian Prime Minister Sadat in Washington under President Jimmy Carter. Memories of peace and war intermingled again.

During the traditional Sabbath text study session at the conference, author Naamah Kelman—director of the Department of Education of the Israel Movement for Progressive Judaism—showed us from a terrace of Hebrew University the actual path where the Yom Kippur scapegoat was led into the wilderness to atone for the tribal sins during the Sinai wandering. Here was one more element to relate to my Buddhist experience. I thought of the lama-dancing and the burning of obscurations, formerly done (in the indigenous Bön religion of Tibet) with animal sacrifice like that of the Temple Jews, as a ritual of spiritual cleansing. In one study group, comments were made reinforcing the stereotype about Buddhists withdrawing from the world into their own inner search for enlightenment, as contrasted with the Jewish commitment to action and good deeds. Both traditions, I kept thinking, have both contemplation and action; but this still didn't make me feel at home with myself.

The braided-candle ritual called Havdalah, embodying the separation of the sacred from the secular, takes place at sunset, ending the Sabbath. This one had hundreds of spirited participants on a large patio overlooking the lights of the city. On such a height as this in ancient times did two witnesses wait to sight the first stars of evening; they would then run with their testimony to the rabbinical Sanhedrin council, who then announced the Sabbath's end and performed this ceremony to begin the work week. Since the Jewish year is determined by the lunar calendar, the stars and the moon have played a large role in determining festival days as well as secular dealings.

The Sabbath brought me a piecemeal escape from my urgency, but a Sunday outing to Haifa—Boston's sister city and Israel's most integrated city—reminded me of the sad polarization of secular liberal Jews against Israeli Orthodox Jews around the controversial issue of "Who is a Jew?" I again hoped that the healthy dialogue of various viewpoints at CAJE could be transferred everywhere.

We stopped at an Israeli absorption center for Jewish immigrants from other countries. I noticed the Ethiopians in particular, who, because they were cut off from the rest of the world's Jews before the writing of the Talmud, essentially lived the Mosaic way of life as indicated in the Torah. Most of the early arrivals had to undergo insulting conversion rituals. However, here I was inspired by the language, occupational, and cultural training of Ethiopians side by side with Russians, striking up their first allegiances. At a shop selling Ethiopian crafts, called Beit ha-Yotzer (House of Creation), north of Acco, I was struck by the grace of the Ethiopian clerks and the exotic ceramic figures and striking embroidery work. Their crafts and artwork spoke of that pre-Talmudic time when my people wandered in the desert. I wondered what their Torah chanting sounded like; I imagined that it was resonant with the memory of Mosaic times.

Upon my return to Hebrew University, I scoured the catalogue of classes and elected the sessions about my beautiful dark-skinned cousins with classical features. In his book *The Falashas: The Forgotten Jews of Ethiopia*, David Kessler describes how they practice a pre-rabbinical form of Judaism; their ancient origin in Ethiopia antecedes both the Christians and Muslims. Persecuted in the land of their birth for "killing Christ," they preferred to be called Beta Israel, meaning "House of Israel," instead of the derogatory "Falasha," meaning landless, wanderer, stranger. The tribe reportedly began with the union of the Queen of Sheba and King Solomon, after which the queen converted to Judaism and bore a son, Menelik. Legends telling how the lost Ark of the Covenant was left for safekeeping with Menelik after his visit to his father, Solomon, sparked a warmth in me. Beta Israel strictly adheres to the Torah but not to the later oral law of the rabbis, hermeneutically codified and compiled into the Talmud around 500 CE, because they were cut off from Jews from the rest of the world. Ethiopian Jews were generally not scholars but agriculturists, and they are, according to Kessler, "eager to be instructed" in the Talmud.

In 1973, the Chief Sefardic Rabbi of Israel, Ovadia Yossef, declared that they were, indeed, from the Tribe of Dan, and thereby allowed to emigrate to Israel under the Law of Return. This was, however, during the political upheaval following the Yom Kippur War, when Ethiopian diplomatic relations became difficult. Finally, in January 1985, "Operation Moses" secretly airlifted fifteen thousand Ethiopian Jews to Israel; in crowded, seatless airplanes they sat on the floor, quiet, dignified, and dressed in their best white clothes for their long-awaited return. A struggle about their legitimacy continues with the Israeli rabbinate.

This history intrigued me, and I questioned whether these people, who were closer to mysical, pre-Talmudic times, had a monastic and meditative tradition. Ethiopians kept to the early biblical way of life, complete with some practice of sacrifice, and so were closer to the original Judaism than anyone alive today.

My questions were answered in a session led by Shoshana Ben-Dor, Director of the Israel office of the North American Conference on Ethiopian Jewry. I learned about a Beta Israel monk named Aba Mahari who had led a failed attempt to bring some members of the community to Israel in 1862. A monk? Perhaps this monastic tradition included a knowledge of meditation! Maybe I was getting closer to finding something significant—or maybe I was fooling myself in my search for similarities. This monastic tradition seemed similar to the Tibetan system, where devotees enter the order for a time and then reenter the world of familial responsibilities after their retreat. Shoshana even related how, before Operation Moses, a tribal elder found a rare red heifer and, as described in the Torah, burned it and used the ashes to purify the tribe before entering the Holy Land.

Perhaps there was still a monk alive now. I hoped to interview an Ethiopian spiritual leader and hear some Torah chanting, although their languages—Ge'ez (prayerbook religious language) and Amharic (the official language of Ethiopia)—were beyond me. I was feeling as if I had betrayed my own tradition by my Buddhist spiritual experiences, and needed to find similar resources in this Israel pilgrimage. I even took an excursion to Beersheba to see the new Ethiopian synagogue, but it was closed when I arrived. I did see a *mikvah*, a facility for Jewish ritual immersion, being constructed, which provided evidence of a lively growing community here.

So far I had some clues, but still nothing comparable to my Buddhist experiences.

CAJE participants took study outings to every significant town, city, and settlement all over Israel including Safed, Masada, the Judean Desert and Ein Gedi, the Golan Heights and Tel Aviv, and Tel Arad near the Dead Sea. Individuals, families, tribes, agencies, and institutions were visited, including old rabbinical families and new immigrant families, ultra-Orthodox Jews and politically liberal Israelis. With the historical, political, spiritual sides of Jerusalem available to us through experiential and classroom study, I chose to examine Jerusalem's artistic life for inspiration. Standing before the vista of Mount Scopus, my group's guide read Yehudah Amicai's poem "Ecology of Jerusalem," with its memorable line "The air over Jerusalem is saturated with prayers and dreams." This was certainly a far cry from the industrial smog of Kathmandu.

We visited the studios of an artistic woodcarver who goes by the name of Catriel. He showed us his miniature re-creation of the second Temple—a dollhouse version of the focus of my spiritual journey, the Holy of Holies! In his fan-blown but humid studio, Catriel lovingly quoted Talmud and Torah to confirm that the structure he had built so painstakingly was close to the source. I imagined barefoot pilgrims coming with their offerings. (There even was a CAJE workshop enacting these offerings through the streets of Jerusalem's Old City to the Kotel.)

In another synchronicitous act, I asked about the chair in his display window; it was a replica of the famous chair of Rabbi Nachman! This great master meditator and storyteller had left no successor, so his chair is kept empty in his followers' synagogue. After the Second World War, the chair was smuggled out of his court, piece by numbered piece, to be reassembled, and Catriel was chosen as worthy of this devotion. Pilgrims—two thousand from Israel alone in twelve chartered planes—travel every Rosh ha-Shanah to Uman, Ukraine, to make a pilgrimage to the grave of this master who taught that prayers are the mantras through which one joins with the Ayn Sof.

Juxtaposed to these inspiring events, I visited the site of the Rabin assassination, Tel Aviv's Rabin Square, where I contributed my memorial poem to its graffiti. Then I entered Independence Hall, where a recording of the 1948 Declaration of Independence echoed through the large room in Ben-Gurion's voice, the same declaration that I heard read to that Detroit crowd in the field. Then it meant peace, and now, in a roller-coaster ride to the present, it reminded me of present struggles—again!

Neither Tel Aviv, nor Haifa, nor even beloved Jerusalem had satisfied my search.

16

In the Desert

So far I had only encountered intuitive glimpses connecting my heritage with my son's spiritual path and my personal experiences with his teachers. Perhaps, I thought, I could find the epiphany I sought in the desert, so I took a bus south to Kibbutz Ketura. I hoped to touch that first spark of inspiration in my teenage dream of being a pioneer on a kibbutz that had made the desert bloom.

During the long ride down, I reviewed the disjointed nature of my visit thus far. As I became more discouraged, the August heat weighed down my sleep-deprived body and my tired spirit. Maybe, I thought with a scowl, I was yoking two opposites into an unnatural union that didn't exist. Maybe, I doubted even further, I just couldn't tolerate this wear and tear anymore. Maybe this was a hopeless quest. As we drove by the Dead Sea, Jordan's mountains cast shadows toward me with the black outline fabled to resemble the King of Arabia on his stallion.

Intermittently, I dozed, awakened, read, asked myself more questions, and dropped into unconsciousness. Discouraging thoughts, about my failing and aging body parts with a full history of old associations, made me wish for the resurrection of youth. Maybe I dozed; maybe I hallucinated, projected, envisioned, or invented what I heard next.

Whatever it was that spoke, the words it carried startled me.

"Let it go through you."

Who whispered this softly into my ear? I could hear a slight wind that felt as light as feathers brushing my cheek, or maybe it was a rustle of fabric from my seatmate. But no, that was not it. It was definitely a meditation instruction, but whose? Was I talking to myself? Was it a fragment of overheard conversation on the bus? Intense air-conditioning can float anything toward you, but maybe if we hear voices, it is the soul doing ventriloquist tricks to fabricate an exterior comfort in the face of an interior lack of hope. Was it an angel? One of the fabled thirty-six *tzaddikim*, those holy, dedicated souls living in the world always? Some mystic resident soul of Israel, some Elijah assigned to guide this wayward, serendipitous soul? Perhaps . . . my mother?

Regardless of its reality or source, I would return to this instruction repeatedly in times to come.

Wide awake and unmindful of any fatigue, my seatmate pointed to Mount Nebo, where Moses unsuccessfully pleaded with G-d for entrance to the Holy Land. Why me, and why now, I thought, and not him? I kept asking this question all during my time at the kibbutz and later, when a kibbutz guide took us to Timna in the south Negev Desert where the primordial rock had risen to leave almost mountainous plates. Here I got a taste of the Israelites' forty-year desert wandering, the same desert that housed Jesus' forty-day retreat. Our study group read from the Bible and from modern writers on the desert, like Rabbi Lawrence Kushner; in his *Honey from the Rock* he calls the wilderness "a way of being" where "you see the world as if for the first time." We discussed, we climbed, we took pictures, and then we were set loose onto the plain itself.

I walked far from the group, very far, far enough so that my walking meditation would not be noticed against the long landscape. Slowly I stirred the minuscule grains of sand sifting across the plains of my psyche. Slowly I turned and slowly I sat down in meditative posture to face where I had come from. I seated myself under some solitary tree and listened. Here I was, the classic wandering Jew in the wilderness, seeking to be cleansed, to become whole, to touch the Holy of Holies, and to come home again to myself in this holy heartland.

Alone I was not lonely.

In the distance I could see Solomon's pillars, reminding me of my craving for a moment of Divinity below the Western Wall's Herodian rock. Only these rising rock formations were not hand-hewn; they were made by more powerful forces. I began a meditative gaze as a shimmer rose above the earth's outlines. Silence is like our own breath in the desert, where the wind is warmer than our body and strangely comforting. The sun did not bother or bake me. I heard the wind sigh like the elongated sound of *Eh-he-yeh,* again and again, *Eh-he-yeh* (the Divine Name sometimes translated "I Am That I Am"). It was the sound of my own history breathing my life back to me. I could hear it; I could feel it; this was no hallucination and there was no startle or question. There was no mind thinking. Peace was no further away than my own heartbeat. The desert and the mountaintop had the same vibrations, the valley and the hilltop, the water and the land.

Today I was lucky. Time floated in its own dimension and was enough; it was just long enough when I was called back to the group.

My last night in Israel, I couldn't leave the Kotel Plaza even though outside the Old City wall in the wadi there was an international festival where a band from Ghana might have made an interesting climax to my visit. But it was not as interesting as the puzzling pull to pace this stony expanse. I had just come from a rest stop in Heritage House, where my daughter's friend Susie Schneider, the evening manager of this woman's hostel once managed by my daughter, was advising a sojourner about a breath-based meditation using the name of G-d.

The idea is to have the name always in your mind and in your heart, just like the commandment which says that it "shall be

upon your heart . . . while you sit in your home, while you walk
on the way, when you retire and when you arise" (Deuteronomy
6:6). I was reminded of Rabbi Nachman's teachings to be in continual prayer like an unending mantra. Synchronicity can be con-
firming sometimes.

In the open air, I watched the city's stones slowly turn golden in
the sunset. I waited for the dewy cool of the late evening in a chair
that I had claimed for my duration at the Wall. The voice of the
muezzin called our Semitic cousins to the evening prayer from the
minaret above the Dome of the Rock and cut through the quiet
murmuring cacophony of Jewish prayers whispering at the Wall
below. This mosque is said to rest on the place where Abraham
bound and almost sacrificed his son Isaac, the subject of Ben's bar
mitzvah speech, and also on the original site of the Holy of Holies
in Solomon's Temple; it is also reported to be the site of Muham-
mad's "Night Journey" to G-d after being awakened by the angel
Gabriel. It is not to the wall, I now reminded myself, that we pray
but through it, to the Holy of Holies. This Western Wall that once
retained the Temple Mount and its expanded Herodian enclosure
also holds the home of the G-d we know as YHVH.

Midnight drew me to walk, yes meditatively, toward the Wall
as the numbers of the devotees thinned. I could feel the stones
below my feet and the warm breeze floating my long dress. I held
my unopened prayerbook as I caressed the worn boulders and
took up my ancestral mantra, the Shema, the central Jewish
prayer declaring G-d's Oneness. Then I opened the prayerbook
and prayed the entire evening service. The heart of the prayer service acknowledges the Sustainer of Life with Loving-Kindness,
the Resurrector of the Dead. I whispered to the stones and laid
myself against them and heard the murmuring of all the prayers
before me, beside me, and the prayers of those not yet come.

The hum of life, maybe it emanated from the inside, and maybe
it was in tune with the surroundings—this was my music, the harmony that makes my tear ducts open. I was home and prayed my
own prayer now:

I am the Rock, bursting
In this, Your Place of Rocks,
Of stones standing on the shoulders
Of other stones,
A wall whose words rise up
From the sealed bonds of memory;
They sing, spread, and fly
Like the preened wings of courting birds
Who search the landscape for such love,
And nest within that bright bush
Whose roots hold the heart of the wall.
New songs of prayer rise up to You.
They plead for us;
I pray they multiply.

Your rocks are wailing,
A chorus of blues-singers
Skit-skatting up the scale
From their bottom-base,
From their pit of this old-time ruin.
They tell of Temple-times, and by those tales,
They climb to heights
Beyond the peaks of turrets.

The wall grows bright and brighter at each round,
And we, the children of these prayers,
Join this reach and blend
With the sun and moon and stars and clouds.

We are the wall, growing from our past;
We are the birds who roost and flutter here;
We hover in this sweet peak of light.
We are Your choir of people,
Moving, note by note,
Rebuilding rock by pillar,
To become ourselves again.

O Holy One of Prayer,
Hear us sing.

Hear us sing.

In spite of my anxieties about all the transfers that lay ahead, I boarded a bus. No cab would take me very far. I announced my destination to other passengers; one by one, I received their cautions, opinions, guidances. At the transfer, one took my hand and another crossed the street with me. On the next bus, someone else shouted out my stop, and another took me to the door. I was safe and sound. After all, the whole country was home to my personal revival of spirit.

17

~~

The Unutterable Name of G-d

SITTING WITH FIFTEEN OTHER PARTICIPANTS, I AM INTON-
ing the four letters of the secret name of G-d. If not for my Buddhist experiences, I never would have been motivated to unearth
these meditative groups in Jewish Renewal. At other sittings this
class has visualized the various colors of the sefirot of the kabbalistic ladder. Today's exercise was a "Kabbalah of Letters" out-
lined by the mystic Abraham Abulafia. This secret name itself has
such power that only its letters are used in this meditation. These
four letters, called the Tetragrammaton, are *yod, heh, vav, heh,*
rendered as YHVH, the English letters that are approximate equivalents of the Hebrew. Since the vowel points are normally not indicated in Hebrew, it is not known how this name was originally
pronounced in ancient times. Sometimes even the Hebrew letters
of this name are not even printed in full, but are abbreviated.

One of the Ten Commandments instructs us not to "take the
name of the Lord in vain," and this injunction is taken very seriously by devout Jews—so seriously that they will utter certain Hebrew names of G-d only during prayer. When mentioning these

names in any other context (as when simply talking about G-d or about the prayer), they commonly substitute another, similar name: for example, HaShem, which literally means "the Name," Adoshem in place of Adonai, or Elokim for Elohim. When devout Jews refer to their own good fortune, they add, "Baruch Ha-Shem," which means "Blessed be the Name."

So holy is the name of Divinity that many Jews, as a reminder that the name is not to be spelled or pronounced, will spell the English word with a hyphen: G-d. I have done so in this book out of respect for this feeling of awe before the Name.

Another interesting Hebrew name for G-d used in the Bible is Elohim. Grammatically plural in form, this name may appear to contradict the Jewish belief in the Oneness of G-d. Rabbi Aryeh Kaplan, in his book *Jewish Meditation*, offers one mystical insight into this puzzle. He quotes a *Zohar* commentary on the following verse of Isaiah 40:26: "Lift your eyes on high, and see who created these, the One who brings out their host by number." The *Zohar* points to two key words in this verse: *mi*, meaning "who," and *eleh*, meaning "these." When these two Hebrew words are combined, their letters spell *Elohim*. Thus, when we contemplate "these"—all the things of the world—and ask "who is the author and basis of these things?" the answer is the one G-d.

Invoking G-d's name in the meditation exercise we were doing was sometimes considered dangerous, but Abulafia was proclaimed the authority in the use of the Divine Names by the leading rabbi in Safed, Moshe Cordevero (according to Aryeh Kaplan in his book *Meditation and Kabbalah*). Even though he warned against dabbling casually in these powerful meditations, Abulafia recorded the Jewish mystical practices first revealed to the biblical prophets and used by the patriarch Abraham; he frequently used them himself. As I joined in with the rest of the class, I earnestly hoped that I was not guilty of dilettantism. Perhaps my shopping in the spiritual marketplace was what had opened me to the frightening spiritual experiences of my past.

Now I pronounced the Hebrew letters very, very slowly. My fellow adventurers and I uttered them again and again, accompa-

nied by our breathing and by head movements touching all four
directions of the compass:

Yod . . . heh . . . vav . . . heh
Yod . . . heh . . . vav . . . heh

As I steadied my breath, I associated to another name: Eheyeh
Asher Eheyeh, the name that YHVH used to identify Himself to
Moses on the desert plain in Exodus 3:14. It is conjugated from
the Hebrew verb "to be," and because of its strange grammatical
form in the present, the past, and the future simultaneously, its
meaning is timeless and mystical. Some translate this as "I am,
was, and will be"; others as "I Am That I Am"; Rabbi Aryeh Kaplan's translation is "I Will Be Who I Will Be." Everett Fox's recent translation renders it, "I will be-there howsoever I will be-
there." To be what you will be could be interpreted as a form of
self-actualization.

This name is the reply to the question of Moses: "When I come
to the Children of Israel and say to them, 'The G-d of your fore-
fathers has sent me to you,' and they say to me, 'What is His
name?'—what shall I say to them?" *Eh-he-yeh.* Like the sound of
wind with all its variations, this sound sometimes raises invisible
hairs on my hands.

The timeless aspect of G-d expressed in the name Ayn Sof, the
One without End, also came to mind. This quality relates to the
highest rung on the kabbalistic ladder, the *sefirah* called Keter, or
Crown, whose color is usually the crystal color of water; it is this
quality that I feel suggests the idea of consciousness without an
object. Keter as the highest rung is the closest that we can come to
Ayn Sof.

Yod . . . heh . . . vav . . . heh

The verb form of this name was used to activate Creation: "Let
there be light." This may have been the same name the prophets
used in their meditations while hidden in the caves. This very

name may have answered Job's challenges from the whirlwind. This was the name that the Kabbalists of Spain and Safed used in their devoted attachment to G-d.

Yod . . . heh . . . vav . . . heh

When the letters are vocalized, the word sounds like wind, like breath coming in and out of our mouth, like the original breath of life. In later transliterations into Greek, Latin, and English, the sound of the name became hardened with each derivative, until in English it became "Jehovah," a safe sound, distant from the original spirit.

This Jewish meditation class was not the first time I had participated in a meditation group, nor would it be the last time. From my early, more turbulent ventures in the late sixties to this peaceful moment, I have to own my own spiritual search, sometimes desperate and sometimes grounded. Sitting there in the echo of my classmates, I promised myself to maintain a stable meditation practice, as best as I could, to strengthen my heart to bear the vicissitudes of life. Without such practice, I had fallen all too often into the valley of fear.

18

Wisdom by Any Other Name

TODAY I AM HOLDING MY MORNING COFFEE, GAZING AT my suburban garden, and meditating on the meaning of my physical home, outside of Boston. I am delighted to watch a hummingbird feeding from my echinacea flower, because, by planting this along with trumpet vine and bee balm, I have finally attracted this quick little flapper, this pointer, smaller than the butterfly floating casually near it, back to me after the thirty-year absence that followed my first sighting of a hummingbird in my yard. I think of the Hebrew blessing thanking G-d for withholding nothing from us and creating beautiful creatures and blossoming trees for our enjoyment. Following this, I turn on a Thich Nhat Hanh tape. There is no logic in my Jewish-Buddhist juxtaposition, just some instinctive spiritual blending.

As I cherish this moment of homely peace with the hummingbird, I blush at the memory of my unabashed breaches of etiquette: my emotion in Jerusalem, my open-eyed staring at that lovely elderly bedridden man in his mountaintop monastery, my quarrels in Plum Village. Is home on a mountaintop, in a desert, or at the Kotel? Or is it here? I remind myself that as long as we are at home with ourselves, any moment can bring us Home.

Even with this comforting thought, my reverie finds me teary-eyed again when I think of what it means to feel that a child has strayed far from home. I know that hummingbirds are easier to attract back than children, but my practice encourages me to give up regret. I have stopped blaming my troubles during Ben's youth for his Buddhism. The philosophy itself is so attractive, gentle, and fruitful that it brings me continual insight from its compassion and methodology. It is no secret that numerous Jews are attracted to the peaceful path of Buddhist transformation. Buddha knew that life is suffering, and he offered a way out of it. Jews certainly know about the continual suffering of life. Perhaps if I were in college again, my insistent curiosity could have led me to the Himalayas. The people who were the political and psychological activists in my youth would probably be on a spiritual quest if they were young again and back in college today.

When I meditate among Buddhists I am asked if I am Jewish, and Jews ask, after hearing this story, how I can maintain my Judaism. If I can hold my Jewish heritage dear, practice meditation, and study Buddhist texts without bowing down to statues, and if I can rename my base of refuge from the Buddha, Dharma, and Sangha, to Ayn Sof, Torah, and Chavurah, then perhaps I could be a Buddhist—if Buddhism claimed to be a religion, which it does not. Buddhism has been taught as a philosophy, which could be followed without rejecting one's hereditary religion. To paraphrase Shakespeare, a rose by any other name still retains its fragrance, or as Gertrude Stein insists, a "rose is a rose is a rose."

I am probably absorbing the philosophy behind Thây's recitation of his poem called "Call Me by My True Names," now being played on tape while I write these words. It tells of Thây's identification with the victim as well as the aggressor and how this merging leads to compassion; he takes on many names in this heartfelt poem. Quoted in *Buddhist America,* he writes, "To practice Buddhism, or to practice anything, we must go back to our roots." In this root of the soul, where, as described by Chayyim Vital, we are attached to G-d, I have no name.

My belief system has been expanded to include the possibility of many approaches to Divinity. Each of us uses our own tribal metaphor to describe, organize, and approach the same basic spiritual phenomenon. I firmly believe this. I also believe that individuals always filter new information through their personal experiences, benchmarks, and belief systems. Essentially by this we are all continually writing our own theology regardless of our heritage, denomination, and lifestyle. I am not straddling two disparate ideals, in spite of the particulars, but rather I choose to deal with my personal experience as a liturgical poet to understand metaphors for existence. Primal Cause notwithstanding, Buddhist meditation finds its Jewish counterpart in *hitbodedut*, spiritual seclusion to gain the faculties to live a more meaningful life, and *hitbonenut*, self-understanding through gazing at natural objects of G-d's Creation.

Even more important than this conclusion, and the underlying commonality of my experiences, there is one great question: how do we get to hear the name of Ayn Sof or what Buddhism calls Mind? And one more question (since Jews always answer a question with another question): once we get to this holy experience, how do we maintain it? In a recent conversation with Mu Soeng, director of the Barre Center for Buddhist Studies, he told me: "Insights and openings are the common heritage of all human beings; everyone has these events in the course of everyday life. The purpose of practice, of training in mindfulness, is to realize their importance and contextualize these openings and insights so that they are not lost."

Each tradition has its own path to redemption and realization. Judaism has *mitzvot*, or commandments, found in the Torah. Judaism also has major denominations within it, the Reform, the Conservative, and the Orthodox formats and many further extensions in the Reconstructionist and followers of the Jewish Renewal movement as well as subdivisions within each of these including liberal Jews bound to repair the world politically as well as Orthodox Jews bound to repair it spiritually. Within the Four Noble Truths and the Eightfold Path, Buddhism has the three main branches of Theravada, Mahayana (including Zen), and Vajrayana, and the new directions of nonsectarian Buddhism, each with its supporting literature and various worldwide centers.

As intricate as synagogue politics are, there are politics in each monastery and each following. Any large spiritual or secular institution has these fragmentations, which help or hinder the path. I'm afraid that once a spiritual experience becomes institutionalized, the group dynamics sometimes, unfortunately, resemble the power struggles found within the corporate world.

Mystical Judaism has many approaches to clearing our consciousness to merge with Divinity; Buddhism likewise has its methodology for taming the mind. Kabbalistic imagery uses the *sefirot* of the ladder of attributes to enlightenment, or Ruach ha-Kodesh, the Holy Spirit, as described by the prophet Elijah. Jewish teachers have used Ezekiel's chariot, the letters of the Hebrew alphabet, and the letters of the Tetragrammaton as focuses for meditation. Likewise Buddhists can concentrate on the breath, on colors, or on divine images representing various traits as part of their discipline. Unfortunately, the doors to the Jewish meditation experience were closed by the nineteenth-century Jewish Enlightenment, which stressed intellectual accomplishments and regarded mysticism as superstition, by the elimination of Jewish masters in the Holocaust, by exclusivity, and by fear of the dangers of meditation. Even though new revivals are nearby, more doors will be opened in the future.

One Pali text that I studied at the Barre Center for Buddhist Studies was called the *Dantabhumi Sutta* ("The Grade of the Tamed"); it uses the metaphor of taming a wild elephant to illustrate how the mind is like an uncivilized beast that needs to abandon covetousness, ill will, sloth and torpor, restlessness and remorse, as well as doubt, in order to be still. To bring merit to the world through full awareness, one must purify the mind to endure life's travails in order to live more fully. While the stereotype of the Buddhist monk who withdraws to "study his navel" describes only selfish ends, less is popularly known of the Mahayana ideal of the Bodhisattva, the person who vows to forgo his or her enlightenment until all sentient beings are enlightened. In reality, Buddhists direct their intentions to be of use in the world, sometimes becoming healers and administrators for their secular community.

The elephant metaphor reminds me of another story, the one about the wise men and the elephant. I use it as a parable for my personal theology. A king assigned his wise men to study the elephant, since it was the most useful beast of burden at that time. However, since each one was blind, each described the elephant from his own position or perspective, so one said that the elephant is like a thin tail, another said it was like a large ivory tusk, another described the elephant as a long, rough, and flexible trunk, and so on. We are each like the blind person groping for Divinity, each insisting that the Ultimate Experience is a projection of our own viewpoint—the most familiar, most particular, and therefore most limited experience. I don't exclude myself from this; I too am blindly groping, in piecemeal fashion, toward awareness. Although I have cultivated the richness of my heritage, I can use all the help I can get. Although Jewish mothers have been blamed for their offsprings' ills and much maligned by novelists, psychotherapists, and TV sitcoms, I am just a simple Jewish mother seeking wisdom by any name.

My son's Plum Village friend Sister Lödre, who entered the order after raising her children, said to me that we are all climbing our own path to the mountaintop. When we all arrive, we can then look back to see the other paths that have served the same purpose. In *Pirkei Avot*, a classic Jewish text, a rabbi asks: Who is wise? And the answer is: The one who learns from all people.

Just as Jacob wrestled with the angel—and was thereafter transformed, earning the new name Israel—it is my karma to constantly wrestle with my belief systems and my spiritual rituals. I thought that if I practiced Judaism according to my heart, my children would follow; that has been true two out of three tries. Because Ben has chosen a path different from mine, or different from the wishes that I had for him, does not mean that I can treat him as "the other." As they bring home new ideas, my children have constantly forced me to rethink basic beliefs. Every tradition honors parents, but little is said about honoring children, who the Buddhists say may have been our parents in previous lifetimes. If the moment carries all, our past, our present, and our future, as the Hebrew name of G-d implies, then our children make us face our past in the present moment and bring us a new dimension of that future. Perhaps spiritual DNA is another kind of karma.

This life is just a heartbeat in the pulse of eternity, but it contains a spark of the Larger Light, and could spark again at some other time and place. Ben and I could return or not return again to the same locus. He could be my nephew, my brother, my father, but perhaps not my son again. By some theories of reincarnation, it was he who chose me to help him fulfill this life's mission. I believe it's my job to help him, or at least to love him unconditionally. I'm doing the best I can, and if he hears a different drummer, maybe I have to learn that beat.

Sometimes my meditation brings thoughts of the third millennium with its new and emerging spirituality. In the past, Judaism, like Buddhism, has been influenced by contemporary events and new neighbors. As technological communication advances, our world is becoming increasingly smaller, and this global village that we call home will be seeking new syntheses of belief. This is destiny, not prophecy, because religions, civilizations, and people have influenced each other throughout history. A better book than mine will surely be written about this phenomenon in the new millenium. I look forward to reading it in my old age.

Meanwhile, my own interpretation of a classic Jewish story about what the Buddhists call enlightenment has been influenced by my journey to meet my son's Asian teachers.

The Talmud tells of four rabbis—Ben Azzai, Ben Zoma, Elisha ben Abuya, and Rabbi Akiva—who entered Pardes, translated as the "Orchard," meaning the Garden of Eden. Pardes in this story could symbolize the mystical experience in Ezekiel's vision in Ezekiel 10:5, usually considered the cornerstone and beginning point of the study of Jewish mystical visions. In any event these, I believe, are the Jewish metaphors for spiritual experience. The story tells how these famous sages reacted to their experience. Ben Azzai died. Ben Zoma went mad. Elisha ben Abuya became an apostate. Only Rabbi Akiva entered in peace and left in peace. Why? Rabbi Akiva warned his friends: "When you enter near the stones of pure marble, do not say, 'Water, water,' since it is written, 'He who speaks falsehood will not be established before My eyes' (Psalm 101:7)."

It took a long time for me to unpack this and arrive at conclusions that made sense to me. The four rabbis had enlightenment experiences, and Akiva, by his warning, was their teacher in this journey. Only Akiva knew how to handle it. His reference to water recalls Keter, the highest *sefirah*, or rung on kabbalistic ladder ascending to enlightened awakening; its color is clear like water. The form of the vision in this story is stones of pure marble. However, it is still a vision, a metaphor, a vehicle like a chariot, so that we, in our manifest form, can see this experience. To name it as a real phenomenon is to lie, as Psalm 101 implies. The quest for a sustained state of enlightenment was a failure for the other three rabbis, who were unprepared to hold the experience in mindful meditation because they clung to that experience. Rabbi Akiva, as the voice in my dream on the Israeli bus instructed, let it go through him. The practice of mindful meditation understands that visions transform under meditative observation. Even scientists know this today. Consider the Heisenberg principle, which states that the object of scientific observation changes just by virtue of the act of observation.

I know that not all readers will agree with me. Even for me these self-constructed paradigms do not help in my moment-to-moment life or my individual path. I still have to confront my mistakes with myself and my family when I come to the yearly summary of misdeeds at the High Holy Days, or when I sit and try to focus on the breath, or even when I design meditation approaches for my workshops. But when I write, when I am asked to produce a poem for a prayerbook or anthology, those are the moments where my words go before my experience and tell me how fearful

I am of Divinity, of awakening, and of realization. If I arrive, perhaps I will fail like some of Rabbi Akiva's students. Perhaps I will be distracted by false, self-aggrandizing ideas.

It's scary even to begin, let alone continue, this spiritual quest to bring these disparate elements of my life into one common denominator. It is as scary and sometimes as painful as bringing children into the world and watching a transformation that is beyond their primal beginning. By their suffering they remind us of the mistaken actions that we have committed. They rise up like the future to challenge us. Peace with them is only, as Thây says, in the present moment.

I sometimes wish that I could be as silent as the first letter of the Hebrew alphabet, the Alef itself. This letter, sometimes the focus of visualization in Jewish meditation, became the inspiration for a poem to ground myself, to begin to begin, to pray or to meditate—all synonymous with one another. Writing this liturgical poem in the seventies was an act of meditation for me, because my words go before me like prophecies; unlocking my own secrets from myself, they tell me how I feel; they describe the beginning at all ends.

THE ALEF-BET OF PRAYER

Let me not be afraid of Your letters,
All fire, all brimstone;
Without parchment, without bone,
They are as fleshless, as I am alone.

They breathe, and I hear that formless echo
Sparking images of the first Creation.
They move, and all sensation becomes
A silent rush toward the curved embrace of time.

If I could close my eyes and remember You,
Who can light a bush and not consume,
Who with Your Fingers can make the tablets bloom
With holiness, I could draw warmth from stone,

Or better yet, a rock, I could get honey
From a rock, I could wrestle with an angel,
Know my true name and not fall a victim
To this wall of chatter. An easy prayer

Would be a bridge to You, my Source, My Love.
Help me curl my mouth around that seed.
I've lost my youth in search of inspiration;
Give me the power of the first Alef,
The soundless sound before the first word,
The first word that was wind,
And the first silence
Before my long journey into meaning.